GREAT AMERICAN
ROAD TRIPS
Scenic Drives

Morning light approaches beneath Handies Peak in Colorado's San Juan Mountains.

▼

Wildflowers bloom near Kenai Lake in Alaska.

EXECUTIVE EDITOR Kirsten Schrader
ASSOCIATE CREATIVE DIRECTOR Christina Spalatin
DEPUTY EDITOR Marija Andric
SENIOR ART DIRECTOR Kristen Stecklein
EDITOR Julie Kuczynski
COPY EDITOR Ann Walter
PRODUCTION COORDINATOR Jon Syverson
SENIOR RIGHTS ASSOCIATE Jill Godsey

PICTURED ON FRONT COVER
Linn Cove Viaduct, North Carolina,
Sean Pavone/Shutterstock

ILLUSTRATION Anna Simmons

ADDITIONAL PHOTO INFORMATION
Page 6: Bandon Beach, Oregon
Page 56: Monument Valley Navajo Tribal Park, Arizona
Page 78: Eagle Harbor Lighthouse, Michigan
Page 110: Linn Cove Viaduct, North Carolina
Page 144: Cape Cod, Massachusetts

© 2020 RDA Enthusiast Brands, LLC.
1610 N. 2nd St., Suite 102
Milwaukee, WI 53212-3906

INTERNATIONAL STANDARD BOOK NUMBER
978-1-62145-523-3 (Hardcover)
978-1-62145-524-0 (Paperback)

LIBRARY OF CONGRESS CONTROL NUMBER 2020944249

COMPONENT NUMBER 116500100H

CONTENTS

*A pink sky is cast ◄
as the sun sets
over farmland in
Vermont. Mount
Mansfield is seen
in the distance.*

Evening clouds roll over Captain Jack's Wharf at Provincetown Harbor in Massachusetts.

TERRY DONNELLY

COME ALONG FOR THE RIDE!

LET THE NATURAL BEAUTY of America's most scenic drives inspire the travel bug within you and get you out exploring wide-open spaces and breathtaking vistas. These trips will take you on an odyssey in your car, van or RV. Whether you're an armchair traveler or ready to pack and roll, this first book in our new *Great American Road Trips* series covering *Scenic Drives* has exactly what you are looking for.

All accounts here are firsthand from the travelers and photographers themselves, with helpful added tips. Some drives are more leisurely, like Cape Cod's Route 6 in Massachusetts (page 160), which will lead you to exquisite sandy beaches and charming shops. Others, like Cathy and Gordon Illg's trip along North America's highest paved road, the Mount Evans Scenic Byway in Colorado (page 22), are for the more adventurous, or as they put it: "…just because you can drive up to this rarefied atmosphere doesn't mean you don't have to earn it."

Just imagine, as you take on these routes, the ingenuity that went in to creating them and how much more difficult it would be to traverse the terrain without these modern wonders of roads.

So meander through the spectacular scenery, and don't forget to take photos along the way! For now, sit back, relax and enjoy the ride!

—FROM THE EDITORS

ALASKA

WEST

WASHINGTON

MONTANA

OREGON

IDAHO

WYOMING

NEVADA

UTAH

COLORADO

CALIFORNIA

HAWAII

▼

The Resurrection River curves below Mount Benson.

STORY BY **JANINE NIEBRUGGE**
PHOTOS BY **RON NIEBRUGGE**

SEWARD HIGHWAY

TRAVEL 127 UNFORGETTABLE MILES THROUGH ONE OF NORTH AMERICA'S MOST PRISTINE WILDERNESSES.

DESIGNATED BOTH A National Forest Scenic Byway and an All-American Road, the Seward Highway takes you through 127 miles of remote wild beauty.

Also known as Alaska Route 9, the highway stretches from Anchorage to the charming coastal community of Seward, the gateway to Kenai Fjords National Park.

The road climbs over mountain passes where you're surrounded by jaw-dropping views of jagged peaks, rainforests, crystal lakes and the Pacific Ocean.

On any given day, you're likely to see Dall sheep, whales, waterfowl, moose and bears. What you won't see are billboards or many other signs of civilization.

The highway is a photographer's dream, with easy access to dramatic scenery. While it's not hard to complete the drive in a few hours, give yourself

most of a day, or even two, to explore this stunning road.

To guide you along on your journey, here are a few of the highlights that my husband, Ron, and I enjoy.

As you start out, Potter Marsh, on the outskirts of Anchorage, marks the end of city views and the beginning of wilderness. It's truly a birder's paradise, with views of a rich variety of waterfowl and other birds, including northern pintails, Canada geese, red-necked phalaropes, canvasback ducks, horned and red-necked grebes, and northern harriers. Gulls, arctic terns and yellowlegs can be spotted during spring and fall migration. This is also a good place to see spawning salmon and an occasional moose.

As you continue down the highway, wind your way along the Turnagain Arm, with scenic views of Chugach State Park. Turnagain Arm offers

POINTS of INTEREST

LENGTH
127 miles

FUN FACT
The five massive glaciers in Portage Valley on Turnagain Arm are remnants of Portage Glacier, which once covered the valley's entire 14-mile length.

SIDE TRIP
Two miles north of Seward, turn west onto a gravel road that parallels the Resurrection River for 9 miles. The road ends at the Exit Glacier Ranger Station in Kenai Fjords National Park.

A 3-mile-long river of ice flowing from massive Harding Icefield, Exit Glacier looms like a blue monolith. Visitors can approach the glacier's base by walking about a half-mile on an easy trail from the ranger station. A longer, more strenuous trail leads hikers up the flank of the glacier to a spot overlooking the Harding Icefield.

The mantle of ice measures an imposing 35 miles by 20 miles, and buried within its frigid bulk are all but the tallest peaks to be found in the Kenai Mountains.

▼
A bull moose crosses the road in Chugach National Forest.

some of the world's largest bore tides, attracting surfers, paddleboarders and kite boarders.

Ron and I like to stop at Beluga Point or Bird Point to watch for beluga whales and scour the mountainsides along the road for Dall sheep.

Milepost 79 is the turnoff for the skiing community of Girdwood, a quaint mountain town that's worth exploring. If you have time, take a hike on the Winner Creek Trail. Winner Creek is a beautiful, clear-running stream flowing through the rainforest. A little farther up, the creek drops into a steep, narrow, rocky gorge. You'll want to stop and enjoy the view.

This milepost is also your last opportunity for gas and any other supplies you might need until you reach Seward.

As you continue down Turnagain Arm, check out Portage Valley, a

14-mile isthmus that connects the Kenai Peninsula to the mainland.

Going farther, you'll find yourself climbing Turnagain Pass into the heart of the Chugach National Forest. Here you'll be treated to towering snowcapped peaks, lush rainforest, rivers, lakes and ponds.

Traveling through the communities of Moose Pass and Crown Point will make you feel like you've taken a step back in time. Stop to take in the beauty of the turquoise waters of Kenai Lake, and look for nesting trumpeter swans in the lily pad pond at Mile 15.

The drive ends as you enter the charming seaside community of Seward, with views of Resurrection Bay. Take a boat tour to watch for humpback and orca whales, sea otters and sea lions in Kenai Fjords National Park—the perfect way to end a great road trip. ◗

▼

Autumn glows in Chugach National Forest on the Kenai Peninsula.

The picturesque Santa Lucia Mountains line the Big Sur coast.

STORY AND PHOTOS BY
LONDIE GARCIA PADELSKY

BIG SUR COAST

SHEER CLIFFS, HAIRPIN TURNS AND MAJESTIC OCEAN VIEWS MAKE THIS COASTAL ROUTE A THRILLING RIDE.

CALIFORNIA'S STATE ROUTE 1, also known as the Pacific Coast Highway, stretches along some of the most beautiful coastline in the world. The highway runs virtually the entire length of the state, but my favorite stretch is the Big Sur section from San Simeon to Carmel, which is so stunning that it is a designated National Scenic Byway.

As you drive north from San Simeon, the highway makes its first ascent to Ragged Point Vista, where you come face to face with the ruggedness and steepness of the Santa Lucia Mountains as they rise up along the ocean. For those of us with a fear of heights, there's comfort in driving north, hugging the mountainside.

On the other hand, if you only drive north, you might miss the McWay Falls in Julia Pfeiffer Burns State Park—the only falls in California that empty into the ocean.

I like to camp at Pfeiffer Big Sur State Park, where a walk on the beach leads past the intriguing rock formations known as sea stacks that rise out of the ocean like mysterious towers. The park is also known for its ancient redwoods. Don't miss the chance to hike among some of the world's tallest living trees, soaring 200 to 350 feet into the sky.

Another of my favorite places, just to the north, is Andrew Molera State Park. Here, where the Big Sur River meets the ocean, the mountains flatten out to meadows, and oaks and eucalyptus replace redwoods. I follow the trail along the river to the beach, which is scattered with uniquely crafted beach shelters made of driftwood, rocks and bizarre odds and ends that have washed ashore.

Farther inland, you can spot herds of Holstein dairy cattle grazing in pastures, their familiar black-and-

POINTS of INTEREST

LENGTH
About 90 miles

WORDS TO THE WISE
Rainstorms will sometimes cause landslides. Morning fogs are frequent in summer. Strong currents, cold water and surf along much of the coast make swimming extremely dangerous.

SIDE TRIPS
Point Sur Lighthouse, on the National Register of Historic Places, sits on a volcanic rock 361 feet above the Pacific Ocean. Erected in 1889, the lighthouse has stayed in continuous operation, and is the only complete lighthouse of its era open to the public in California. *pointsur.org*

Sunset Drive swings inland after Asilomar State Beach, passes the well-landscaped grounds of a conference center, then intersects with 17-Mile Drive. Monterey cypresses, gnarled by the wind and ocean spray, are highlights along the toll road, which loops through part of the Monterey Peninsula. Tour maps are provided at tollgates.

▼
Redwood trees along the drive rise to meet the sky.

white patterns making a striking contrast with the background colors.

Continuing north, if you're starting to get sleepy in the flats, the next couple of cliff turns will wake you up. Then comes Bixby Bridge, one of the world's highest single-span bridges. Fortunately there's a big turnout, so you can relax, check out the bridge and safely enjoy the breathtaking view.

At this point I often turn around and head south on the narrow cliff side of the road. The hairpin turns are worth braving because this is a ride you have to experience; words can't describe it.

Once you reach Ragged Point again there are only two more switchbacks, and then the road mellows out. On one trip I cruised past an unexpected herd of elk and then was lucky enough to spot zebras grazing below Hearst Castle, the legendary home of millionaire publisher William Randolph Hearst and one of the state's prime sightseeing destinations.

I'm lucky to live only about 100 miles from this part of the highway. I've driven it often, and I never get tired of it. ✿

▼
Wildflowers bloom on the cliffs above the coastline.

▼
A fisherman has Lake Sabrina and autumn majesty all to himself.

STORY AND PHOTOS BY
LONDIE GARCIA PADELSKY

CALIFORNIA'S U.S. ROUTE 395

VISIT THE EASTERN SIERRA TO EXPLORE GRANITE PEAKS, GOLDEN ASPENS AND ALPINE LAKES.

"THIRTY-FIVE YEARS OF LIVING in the eastern Sierra and I'm as mesmerized by its incredible beauty as though it were my first day traveling through!" I said this out loud to my dog, Buddy, who was sitting beside me on a steep hillside.

We had hiked to this spot at dawn right after a light snow dusting. After two hours, the ground beneath us was almost dry even though the air was still frosty cold.

All week I'd been photographing fall colors while scoping out this particular scene. I was watching an aspen grove, hopeful that all the leaves would turn color at the same time. Now I was waiting for the sun to break through the thick clouds to brighten the yellow and orange leaves on the trees.

Finally, the sun did just that! The aspen trees glistened and glowed in the bright spotlight and in the midst of that moment, surrounded by all

the quietness, it was as though an orchestra were playing.

As the weather forecast predicted, by midmorning the wind was blowing the leaves off the trees into the pelting snow. Buddy and I left just in time and hiked downhill to the road that brought us here: U.S. Route 395.

Originally known as El Camino Sierra (the mountain range road), U.S. Route 395 is a highway that in California stretches about 600 miles north from Interstate 15 in the Mojave Desert community of Hesperia to the Oregon state line in Modoc County.

U.S. Route 395 is designated as a scenic highway from the Inyo-Mono county line to the town of Walker. This is the area I call my homeland—it's the heart of the El Camino Sierra.

From the highway there are exits upon exits that lead to streams, roadside lakes and high country

▼

These two enjoy fly-fishing from a canoe on North Lake.

POINTS of INTEREST

REST STOP
After hiking, biking or kayaking, visit the cafe at Rock Creek Lakes Resort for barbecue and cobbler. *rockcreek lakesresort.com*

SIDE TRIPS
To recharge along the way, take a relaxing soak in one of many natural hot springs in Travertine Hot Springs and Hilltop Hot Springs to enjoy the amazing views!

If you have extra time, Sequoia and Kings Canyon national parks are just a short drive away. The winding Generals Highway neatly connects both parks and travels through Giant Sequoia National Monument, where you can see groves of the massive trees.

trails to the John Muir and Ansel Adams wildernesses. With such easy access to nature's extraordinary getaways, you can hike, bike, fish, ride horseback and climb rocks all in one day—or simply enjoy a secluded picnic.

I treasure all seasons in the eastern Sierra, but am especially partial to fall. I love watching the leaves and desert sages come to life with a rainbow of hues. Red, orange and gold add the most brilliant splash of color on a canvas of gray granite rock walls.

Along U.S. Route 395, fall sets the treetops ablaze first at Bishop Creek Canyon. From Bishop, drive about 12 miles west toward the mountains on California Route 168. At an elevation of 9,000 feet and climbing, here you will enter an autumn dream where aspens sparkle in groves and across steep, majestic mountainsides.

South Lake, Lake Sabrina and North Lake are easy to reach and

boast spectacular reflections from the surrounding peaks, which rise up to 13,000 feet. Fishing streams, trailheads and horseback riding opportunities are scattered in between. In this canyon you can spend a couple of hours or a couple of days, as Buddy and I did.

Soon after the leaf colors have peaked in Bishop Creek Canyon, areas at higher elevations take off full blast. From Bishop, drive north on U.S. Route 395 toward Mammoth Lakes and follow the road signs to more of my fall favorites: Rock Creek, McGee Creek and Convict Lake canyons. Keep in mind that there are campgrounds and restaurants in most canyons, but often no fuel.

At the Mammoth Lakes exit, drive into town and take the scenic gondola to the top of Mammoth Mountain Ski Area. There are no fall trees at this 11,000-foot vista, but you will certainly spot them looking down on the Sierra

▼

Expect a dusting of snow to cover the mountaintops in McGee Canyon.

Londie's dog, Buddy, loves joining her on excursions, and he is well-versed in posing nicely.

McGee Creek is known for its beautiful fall foliage.

Nevada landscape. Just beyond the town, there is a loop road along serene, cobalt blue alpine lakes. Fishermen, paddleboarders, walkers, kayakers and bicyclists enjoy the beauty.

There are more pines than aspens surrounding the Mammoth Lakes Basin loop. For the next big blast of fall colors, continue on the highway to California Route 158. Turn west and follow the vibrant aspens along the June Lake Loop. At the start of the loop road is a stunning view of Carson Peak, perfectly mirrored in crystal clear June Lake. It sets the stage for what's ahead. The two-lane road goes through the small, full-service community of June Lake, and passes several quaint cafes and fishing resorts. The lower hillsides and shorelines shimmer with gold and sparkle in all four glacial lakes: June, Gull, Silver and Grant.

Beyond the June Lake Loop, I like to check out Lundy Canyon, Mono Lake and the panoramic aspen grove on Conway Summit. I often continue up to Bridgeport to photograph the golden grasses in the big meadows with the Sawtooth Range in the distance.

Then I stay on U.S. Route 395 and head to Walker River Canyon, where the water flows by cottonwoods and aspens. It's the perfect scene to take gorgeous photos.

Throughout autumn, you will likely run into Buddy and me in one of these canyons. Just when I start to think the fall color season is over, I drive south on Route 395 to Owens Valley and start taking photos all over again.

A friend once said that from Inyo to Mono County, the fall season on Route 395 is like the staircase to heaven. I wholeheartedly agree. ❧

▼ *Another perfect day dawns on Mount Evans.*

Colorado

STORY AND PHOTOS BY
CATHY & GORDON ILLG

MOUNT EVANS SCENIC BYWAY

TAKE A DEEP BREATH AND ENJOY THE UNMATCHED VISTAS
ALONG AMERICA'S HIGHEST PAVED ROAD.

THE ANIMALS WE WERE TRYING TO PHOTOGRAPH didn't appear to be moving quickly, but they were white dots in the distance within minutes. There was no way we could keep up with them.

Of course, it didn't help that the landscape was straight up and straight down, and that we gasped for breath whenever we tried to walk faster than a stroll. But we weren't complaining.

At 14,000 feet above sea level, we were near the summit of Mount Evans, one of Colorado's fourteeners. We could see the snow-dappled Rockies stretching north, south and west to the horizon. To the east, foothills glowed in the sunrise as they tumbled down toward Denver and the Great Plains beyond.

Spectacular surroundings like these are typically reserved for mountain climbers and long-distance hikers, but the Mount Evans Scenic Byway lets anyone with a car and a reasonable cardiovascular system enjoy the high alpine scenery and the creatures that call it home. The byway, which includes sections of Clear Creek County Road 103 and State Highway 5, climbs more than 7,000 feet.

Construction on the road began in the summer of 1923; eight years later it was open to the public. Workers trudged up the mountain with shovels, hammers, drills and dynamite to blow a path through the rocks. In an area notorious for its heavy weather, they worked through rain, snow and hail. One contractor noted in a report that they "literally forced the work through by hand in spite of every obstacle."

But just because you can drive up to this rarefied atmosphere doesn't mean you don't have to earn it. Highway 5 from Echo Lake to the summit is not for the faint of heart. (Imagine what it must have been like for those early

POINTS of INTEREST

LENGTH
28 miles

FUN FACTS
The road in the sky, Mount Evans highway is the highest paved road in the nation. At more than 14,000 feet up, you'll literally be driving close to the clouds!

Mountain goats are not native to Colorado. The first goats were released in the Mount Evans area in the late 1950s and early '60s. The goats' natural southern range was northern Wyoming.

SIDE TRIP
Estes Park is the eastern gateway to Rocky Mountain National Park and a popular year-round recreational center. The historic Stanley Hotel, a sugar-white grande dame with a red roof, is a popular spot for visitors. It was not only built by F.O. Stanley of Stanley Steamer, it was also the setting that inspired *The Shining,* written by Stephen King.

▼

A mountain goat kid and its mother share a tender moment.

road workers.) The highest paved road in North America, it's also one of the loftiest in the world. There isn't a single section of guardrail along its twisting 14-mile ascent, and it skirts some impressive precipices. For the last 5 miles there's no centerline, and drivers unused to the exposure do tend to hog the middle of the road.

At the edge of the timberline, the road passes through a grove of bristlecone pines. They are the oldest living things in the state. One of the patriarchs of the grove sprouted as the Roman Empire was falling into decline, and their gnarled branches seem to wave goodbye as you leave the trees behind.

The road climbs for 11 more miles without a single tree blocking the view—or the wind. It may be 90 degrees on the prairie below, but it can be below freezing at the top at any time. In fact, the annual mean temperature on the

summit of Mount Evans is 18 degrees, and it's never been warmer than 65. The byway is typically open only from Memorial Day weekend to early October, and sometimes not even that long. Conditions can change at a moment's notice on the mountain. One year early snows closed it down Sept. 3.

The usual assortment of Rocky Mountain critters—marmots, pikas, ptarmigan, mule deer and elk—call Mount Evans home. But it's the bighorn sheep and mountain goats that attract wildlife watchers from around the world. Mountain goats weren't brought to Colorado until the late 1950s, but they have adapted to their new home so well that this is perhaps the best place in the world accessible by car to see them at close range.

If expansive views of alpine wonders or the sight of baby goats playing get your juices flowing, this is the scenic road for you. ◆

▼
Yellow flowers and a blue sky frame this photo of Summit Lake terrifically.

▼
Sunlight paints Mount Sneffels Wilderness Area in the San Juan Mountains.

STORY AND PHOTOS BY
TIM FITZHARRIS

SAN JUAN SKYWAY

ADVENTURE AND FRAGRANT ALPINE WILDFLOWER MEADOWS AWAIT IN COLORADO'S SAN JUAN MOUNTAINS.

FEW ROADS IN THE WORLD offer more beauty and adventure per mile than the San Juan Skyway in southwest Colorado. Along with fabulous alpine views, you'll find historical sites, river rafting, rock climbing, camping, hiking, fishing, horseback riding, mountain biking, high country four-wheeling, spas, hot springs, fine dining, ghost towns and abandoned mines.

The skyway is a 232-mile loop in the shape of a rough triangle, with Cortez, Durango and Ridgway at the corners. While I highly recommend the entire drive, my very favorite section runs along U.S. Route 550 from the iconic cowboy town of Durango to Ouray.

Much of Durango's well-preserved downtown dates back to the region's high-rolling gold mining days in the late 1800s. It's a great place to soak up some atmosphere and gather supplies before heading north into the San Juan Mountains. The fun starts almost as soon as you leave town. Depending on the season, brilliant wildflowers or golden aspens vie with the road for your attention as the drive steadily climbs into the scented wilderness stands of pine and fir of the San Juan National Forest.

Before you know it, you find yourself in open subalpine terrain, winding through one switchback after the next, each offering a new view of the craggy, snow-capped peaks looming above the road and far into the distance. The road climbs through two high mountain passes, Coal Bank and Molas, before arriving in the historic little mining town of Silverton.

Heading north out of Silverton toward Ouray, the road climbs up 11,008-foot-high Red Mountain Pass, then plummets into a heart-in-your-mouth run through Uncompahgre Gorge on the Million Dollar Highway. Built over the course of three years in the 1880s, this monument to human ingenuity hugs sheer rock walls 500 feet above the river. The narrow lanes and lack of guardrails make it one of the most memorable and adventurous drives anywhere.

POINTS of INTEREST

LENGTH
232 miles

FUN FACT
A portion of the road between Silverton and Ouray is known as the Million Dollar Highway. Depending on whom you ask, the highway was named for the amount of gold and silver mined in the area, the value of the low-grade ore tailings used to pave the road, the cost of the construction or the rewarding views.

SIDE TRIP
Grander vistas await beyond the highway. Go off-road and rent a 4x4 or take a Jeep tour in Ouray. *ouraycolorado.com*

NEARBY ATTRACTIONS
Chimney Rock National Monument, west of Pagosa Springs; Lowry Pueblo Ruins, west of Pleasant View; Ute Indian Museum, Montrose; Southern Ute Cultural Center, Ignacio

▼

The appropriately named Red Mountain in Gray Copper Gulch.

While the Million Dollar Highway is perhaps the most exciting section of the skyway, virtually every mile of this high-mountain drive offers great opportunities for photos, sightseeing and daydreaming. Alpine lakes, tarns and streams jeweled with wildflowers flank the road. Distant slopes are spread with aspen and braided with waterfalls; cloud-wreathed pinnacles frame the sky above.

The road also offers access to some of the planet's finest alpine wilderness, easily accessible by foot, horseback or Jeep via a network of trails and mining roads carved through forest and granite mountainside. My favorite off-road destinations are the alpine wildflower meadows that overwhelm the senses in July and August, particularly those at Yankee Boy, American and Governor basins.

Four-wheel it into the backcountry on your own (off-road rentals are available in Silverton and Ouray) or play it safe and join a tour. However you choose to explore this route, you'll have the time of your life. ◉

▼
The West Needle Mountains loom in the distance of the Weminuche Wilderness in the San Juan National Forest.

STORY AND PHOTO BY
LELAND HOWARD

SALMON RIVER SCENIC BYWAY

BLAZE A TRAIL OF PIONEER SPIRIT WITH AMAZING SIGHTS ON THE LEWIS AND CLARK NATIONAL HISTORIC TRAIL.

IDAHO'S SALMON RIVER SCENIC BYWAY begins as Highway 93, crosses the state line from Montana and descends in winding curves through mountain canyons flanked by pines, firs, spruce and cedars. For most of the 161-mile route, the two-lane road follows the main fork of the Salmon River, one of the longest free-flowing rivers in the lower 48 states. A little more than two-thirds of the way down the byway, at Challis, the route veers to the southwest along Highway 75 and ends in Stanley.

It's a 3½-hour drive, but carve out a full day for exploring all the historical sights along the way. In fact, this byway begins at a place called Lost Trail Pass—take it as a sign to lose yourself while you're exploring. The Lewis and Clark exploration party allegedly got disoriented here during its journey from the Mississippi River to the Pacific Ocean in 1804-'06. Much of this scenic drive follows part of the Lewis and Clark National Historic Trail, and many of the views haven't changed.

Salmon's Sacajawea Interpretive, Cultural and Educational Center offers rich insight into the area's natural and native history. Ghost towns like Custer, Bonanza and Bayhorse testify to the gold mining history stemming from the mid-1800s.

After you take the self-guided tour of Bayhorse, I recommend continuing up the canyon. Drive slowly on this steep road and you'll spy a deteriorating cemetery on the hillside. Farther up are structures that once transported ore down and supplies up the extreme incline of the rocky talus slopes.

With views of the Bitterroot Range's White Cloud, Lemhi and Beaverhead mountains, and with glimpses of the Sawtooth peaks between them, plus all the wildlife the Salmon River attracts, you'll find that blazing this pioneer trail will reinvigorate soul and spirit. ◖

POINTS of INTEREST

LENGTH
161 miles

FUN FACT
Hemmed in by sheer cliffs, the dangerous, churning rapids of the Salmon River—a powerful torrent that the Shoshone tribe believed no human could even survive—have earned the waterway the nickname River of No Return. Eventually, however, boatmen learned to master its white water, and today thrilling raft trips and jet-boat tours are available.

SIDE TRIP
Ski the slopes at Lost Trail Ski Area, a family-owned hidden gem with breathtaking views atop the Continental Divide. *losttrail.com*

NEARBY ATTRACTIONS
Painted Rocks State Park, on Route 473 southwest of Hamilton, Montana; Lake Como, nestled in a valley on Como Road northwest of Darby, Montana

▼

As it sinks to the horizon, the sun casts soothing light over the wild Salmon River.

STORY AND PHOTOS BY
CHUCK HANEY

RED SLEEP MOUNTAIN

SUPERB SCENERY, ABUNDANT WILDLIFE AND A BISON HERD MAKE THIS ROUTE ONE OF THE BEST TREKS IN THE WEST.

RED SLEEP MOUNTAIN DRIVE in the National Bison Range winds past some amazing vistas in Big Sky Country. As the 19-mile, one-way gravel road climbs and descends Red Sleep Mountain, every mile reveals a panoramic view.

I often need three or four hours to complete the loop as I like to stop the car and shut off the engine to listen to the melodic songs of the colorful lazuli bunting or the western meadowlark, Montana's state bird.

A series of switchbacks in the road near its 4,885-foot-high point lead to several short hiking trails. At this lofty altitude, Douglas firs and ponderosa pines replace native grasses. It's a good place to see a rambling black bear, whitetail deer or bighorn sheep.

National Bison Range, located between the Bitterroot and Mission mountains, is home to about 350 bison. These 18,500 untamed acres pack in a lot of diverse wildlife including elk, pronghorn antelope, mountain lions, badgers and muskrats, to name a few. And, with about 200 bird species, it's a birding paradise.

The upper stretches of the road are closed from early October to late spring. Prairie Drive, an out-and-back option through the lower "flats," is open all year.

My favorite time to visit is in May, when the road is fully open, the native prairie grasses have greened up and bison calves can be seen following their mothers about.

Traveling Red Sleep Mountain Drive is an adventure that embodies the spirit of the West—independent, rugged and awe-inspiring. ◗

POINTS of INTEREST

LENGTH
19 miles

REST STOPS
Book the lakefront cabin at Swan Hill Bed & Breakfast and start the day with a meal made using fresh local ingredients. *swanhillbedand breakfast.com*

Look for the windmill in the town of Ravalli. There you'll find the best doughnuts around at the Windmill Village Bakery. *windmill villagebakery.com*

NOT TO BE MISSED
Open on Fridays from May to October, the Polson Farmers Market is the place to find local produce, art, baked goods, jams, jellies and more. *polsonfarmers market.com*

SIDE TRIP
Grab your binoculars and be on the lookout for great blue herons, double-crested cormorants and about 200 other bird species at Ninepipe National Wildlife Refuge.

Top: Green grasses make a lovely canvas for bright yellow arrowleaf balsamroot wildflowers. Bottom: Diverse wildlife, including bison herds, is a fixture along the drive.

The rays of a sunset illuminate Haystack Rock at Cannon Beach.

Oregon

STORY BY
DONNA B. ULRICH

OREGON COAST HIGHWAY

NATURAL BEAUTY AND CULINARY ADVENTURES ABOUND WHEN TRAVELING "THE PEOPLE'S COAST."

THE BREATHTAKING VIEWS, forested headlands, sublime sandy beaches and, best of all, accessibility of the Oregon coast make for a scenic drive unlike any other in the country. The ocean is often within sight of the road, which offers easy access to more than 80 state parks and recreation areas.

The Oregon shore truly is "the people's coast," as it's been dubbed. More than 100 years ago, Gov. Oswald West went before the state legislature and successfully argued that the state's entire 363-mile coastline should be established as a public thoroughfare. Construction of what is now Highway 101 soon followed.

In conjunction with this plan, the state's parks department bought land for 36 state parks along the coastal road, an average of one every 10 miles. Tourists soon took advantage of the improved roadways, putting little towns like Depoe Bay and Yachats on the map. In 1967 the legislature passed the Oregon Beach Bill, preserving free beach access for all.

The late Ray Atkeson wrote in his book, *Oregon Coast*, "I realiz(ed) that I was enjoying the privilege of seeing one of the most magnificent stretches of coastline in the world." We met Ray early in our photographic career; his photos influenced my husband, Larry, and me to share his love for the shore.

We are lucky to live only 80 miles from the Oregon border. When we first started traveling and photographing for calendars, magazines and books, images of crashing waves on rugged coastlines sold well, as did lighthouses and sunsets over sandy beaches.

We still like to take off for a few days, camp in the state parks, hike the rugged trails and eat our way up the coast. Try breakfast at the Crazy

POINTS of INTEREST

LENGTH
363 miles

WORDS TO THE WISE
In summer allow plenty of time, since traffic can be heavy and the road is narrow and winding.

SIDE TRIP
For a look at inland scenery, turn east at Gold Beach (29 miles north of Brookings) and follow the 140-mile loop along the Rogue and Coquille rivers. Take Routes 595, 33 and 219 north, then continue on Route 42 from Myrtle Point to Coos Bay. The drive, which passes through a forest containing rare myrtlewood trees, treats travelers to splendid views of cliffs, canyons and the deep blue waters of the rivers.

NEARBY ATTRACTIONS
Tillamook Air Museum; Tillamook County Pioneer Museum; Latimer Quilt & Textile Center, Tillamook; Columbia River Maritime Museum, Astoria

▼

A gate stands open at Fort Clatsop National Memorial.

Norwegians Fish & Chips in Port Orford, a scoop of mudslide ice cream from the Tillamook Cheese Factory, and then a feast of Oregon's only native oysters, the Olympia, in Netarts Bay. These tiny oysters were harvested to near extinction but are now making a very tasty comeback.

After all that eating, we usually need to take a hike. I recommend the trail up to the top of Humbug Mountain near Port Orford. Or head to the Oregon Dunes National Recreation Area, where more than 40 miles of coastline are waiting for your footprints.

Whale-watching is a year-round activity here. Gray whales make their way up the Oregon coast from late March to June and down from mid-December through January. For a week during each peak season, volunteers at 24 sites will help you spot the giant mammals. Larry and I also enjoy bird-watching; when the whales are playing hard-to-get, we'll watch brown pelicans diving for fish or osprey soaring above.

In any season, we like to travel the coast to shoot stunning offshore rock formations called sea stacks. Cannon Beach features the famous Haystack Rock, and the area around the town of Bandon is full of these rock formations. They are especially gorgeous during low tide, when the sunset is reflected in the sand.

Waves crashing on the headlands at Shore Acres State Park, near Charleston, also make for a spectacle— especially from November through January. And near the city of Astoria, the first permanent settlement on the Pacific, you'll find the reconstructed Fort Clatsop, where the Lewis and Clark expedition spent a winter.

Whether you're taking pictures, fishing or watching whales, the Oregon Coast Highway offers an accessible adventure, free of freeways and full of enough beauty to stop traffic. ✺

▼

Humbug Mountain State Park offers a stunning seaside view.

▼
Rushing waters carved the Minam River Canyon, accessible from the western side of the Hells Canyon Scenic Byway.

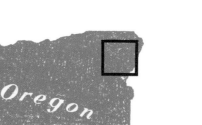

STORY AND PHOTOS BY
DAVID JENSEN

HELLS CANYON

RUGGED LANDSCAPE, ROLLING HILLS AND IDYLLIC FARMS—THIS OREGON ROUTE HAS IT ALL.

BEFORE HELLS CANYON SCENIC BYWAY existed even as an idea, I made several painful, frustrating attempts over the years to follow some of its most primitive segments. The journey never went well, and I often returned home in a vehicle prematurely aged by battles with the rocky, rough track. I always carried two spare tires, and sometimes I needed them both and regretted not having a third. The wonders of Oregon's Hells Canyon, the deepest river gorge in North America, were tantalizingly close and yet so far away.

Then, in 1992, the Wallowa-Whitman National Forest finished paving the 45 miles of primitive track linking the Wallowa Valley with the paved Highway 86 in Baker County. The loop was soon designated as the Hells Canyon Scenic Byway by the U.S. Forest Service. The route I had struggled with was finally on the map in a really big way, eventually becoming an All-American Road and a scenic travel destination.

The byway is at its very best in October, providing access to achingly beautiful autumn vistas along a winding road through coniferous forests, snowy mountains, deep river canyons, and valleys dotted with farms and small towns.

Along the way you will peer right into the plunging depths of Hells Canyon, which was carved over time by the rushing waters of the Snake River. Driving it so late in the season increases the beauty but also the adventure, because you never know when the first big snowstorm will close the high-elevation segment of the route on the east side of the Wallowa Mountains. The forest service cautions that the byway is usually closed due to snow from late October through late May or early June. Timing is important when chasing fall beauty here.

The foliage color intensifies as October advances, reaching its peak late in the month when the reds of huckleberry and hawthorn and the yellows and oranges of cottonwood and larch are at their best, standing out dramatically against the fresh, pristine snow accumulating on the high peaks.

POINTS of INTEREST

LENGTH
213 miles

NOT TO BE MISSED
Mules get the recognition they deserve for carrying loads out west during Hells Canyon Mule Days. Held the weekend after Labor Day in Enterprise, the event promises a Dutch oven cook-off, a parade and more. *hellscanyon muledays.com*

SIDE TRIPS
Follow Highway 86 to the northeast at Pine Creek for an optional side trip to the Snake River at the bottom of Hells Canyon. Carved by the waters of the Snake River, the canyon is deeper than Arizona's Grand Canyon. The road into the canyon and then downstream along the Idaho side of the river is paved to the Hells Canyon Creek Visitor Center. You'll see stunning views of the river winding through stupendous cliffs. This 48-mile round-trip diversion adds two to three hours to the trip.

Hike the trails at the Nez Perce Wallowa Homeland and tour the visitor center to learn about the tribe's history.

Farms with vibrantly colored barns add a peaceful touch to the drive.

Although doing it in eight hours is quite possible, you would get just a sampling of what there is to see. At the start, Highway 84 out of La Grande heads north through farmland along the Grande Ronde River and swings east over Minam Summit, dropping then into the rocky, cottonwood-lined canyons of the Minam and Wallowa rivers. From there, the route follows the Wallowa to its broad upper valley, where snowy mountains stand over a foreground of red barns and where the cottonwoods are brilliant in late October. Fall color also peaks late in the month at Wallowa Lake, a highlight of the drive for many travelers.

Gas up in the tourist town of Joseph, because if you opt for a side trip into the depths of Hells Canyon, your next chance won't come until about 120 miles later at the town of Halfway on Highway 86. From Joseph, a succession of mountain passes through stands of colorful western larch leads to the Imnaha River and then to a final pass where a 2-mile diversion leads to the Hells Canyon Overlook. Then descend south along Pine Creek to Highway 86. Here you will have two options: Turn northeast for the very depths of Hells Canyon (see the side trip at left) or turn southwest toward the town of Halfway.

At Halfway, the byway continues on 86 to the historic Powder River, which led early explorers to the route that came to be known as the Oregon Trail. Flagstaff Hill is the next stop, and there you will find the National Historic Oregon Trail Interpretive Center near I-84 where the byway officially ends.

At the center, reflect on this: From the days of covered wagons until the byway's recent creation, your effortless excursion had been beyond the reach of all but the boldest of adventurers. ●

▼
Mountain peaks dominate the skyline along the road near Enterprise.

▼

Eleven active glaciers comprise Mount Hood's icy coat.

Oregon

STORY AND PHOTOS BY
STEVE TERRILL

MOUNT HOOD SCENIC BYWAY

DELVE INTO FARMLAND AS FAR AS THE EYE CAN SEE, FLOWING WATERS AND ALPINE VISTAS.

HEADING JUST EAST OF PORTLAND, where the Columbia River divides Washington from Oregon, the Mount Hood Scenic Byway offers a breathtaking drive. This nearly triangular loop, roughly 130 miles long, first follows along the Columbia River Gorge, then arcs down and around magnificent Mount Hood.

I start with a piping hot coffee and mouthwatering cinnamon roll from the Troutdale General Store, a homespun gift shop with a nostalgic soda fountain and fun 1950s decor. Merging onto eastbound I-84, I follow the rolling Columbia River. Undulating forested hills, jutting basalt cliffs and rolling grasslands color my view. Union Pacific Railroad tracks snake in and out of sight, promising the sudden excitement of spying a bright yellow locomotive.

So many incredible places branch out along this 50-mile or so stretch, it's hard to pick just one to investigate. In less than an hour's drive, I'll pass 11 state parks and at least as many waterfalls. Between the Sandy River and the Hood River, the highway passes little lakes and crosses many tributaries. There are recreation areas and islands, wildlife refuges and state trails, plus the Bridge of the Gods, Cascade Locks and Bonneville Dam.

But Multnomah Falls, one of the tallest waterfalls in the country, simply cannot be bypassed. Whether you make the short hike to the Benson Bridge or trek the steep 1.2 miles to the top, the view will send your soul soaring.

Onward and eastward, I turn south at the city of Hood River and head into the upper section of the Hood River County Fruit Loop. Here, volcanic soil and moderate climate make this one of the major fruit-producing regions of the world. Roadside stands offer a bounty of local wares: fresh fruits and

POINTS of INTEREST

LENGTH
About 130 miles

FUN FACTS
Steam rising from volcanic vents hint at the magma lurking deep inside the dormant behemoth. National Science Foundation research indicates Mount Hood isn't an explosive eruptor, but more of an oozer.

The volcanic slopes of Mount Hood enrich the rainwater runoff and make the Hood River Valley one of the largest fruit-growing regions in Oregon. Apricots, blueberries, pears, apples and grapes flourish there.

WORDS TO THE WISE
If you are new to mountain climbing, licensed groups like Timberline Mountain Guides and the Northwest School of Survival can teach and guide you.

NEARBY ATTRACTIONS
Hood River and Flerchinger vineyards and Pheasant Valley Winery, Hood River

▼
Cows graze in the pastoral setting of Metzger Prairie.

vegetables, jams, jellies, syrups, wine, baked goods, crafts, antiques and more. Mount Hood looms over this valley of vast orchards, urging me forward, while the reflection of Mount Adams fills my rearview mirror.

Heading south, the road rises and deciduous trees give way to an evergreen forest of Douglas fir. While I follow the Hood River, crisscrossing bridges, the mountain plays peek-a-boo through these trees. Campgrounds dot the forest, with enchanting medieval names like Nottingham and Sherwood Campground. Trails like the Robin Hood Loop lead to wildflower-speckled meadows, waterfall-dotted creeks and other riches.

After rounding the foot of Mount Hood, I detour slightly to the historic 1930s-built Timberline Lodge, a WPA project crafted almost entirely by hand. This National Historic Landmark

features fine dining, snack bars, gift stores, overnight lodging and year-round skiing. The U.S. Forest Service gives an engaging free tour of the lodge and surrounding area.

Finally, I head northwest on Highway 26 back toward Troutdale, winding down the foothills. A pastoral landscape greets me as I emerge from the forest. Small villages here cater to outdoor recreation enthusiasts.

I make one more stop, this time at the Wildwood Recreation Site. After an easy hike along the boardwalk trail, I gaze through a fish-viewing window built into the streambed, amazed by the perspective into underwater life. I'll return to my starting point by nightfall—having spent a full day driving what would take less than three hours without stops. Yet even now, I feel like I could explore so much more! ✦

▼

Multnomah Falls is a popular spot to visit and photograph.

The blue sky here makes a sharp contrast to the Castle, a formation of Navajo and Wingate sandstone.

STORY BY
CATHY & GORDON ILLG

JOURNEY THROUGH TIME

AN ETHEREAL WORLD GLOWS IN GOLD AS FALL ARRIVES IN UTAH'S RED ROCK COUNTRY.

THE FALL COLOR WAS some of the most intense we'd ever seen, and it was in a place few people consider for leaf peeping. It wasn't that the variety of colors was so spectacular, for the leaves were all the same vibrant gold; it was the setting. We were traveling through the desert on the Colorado Plateau in southern Utah.

Our five days without a stoplight, along the 123-mile stretch of state Highway 12 known as the Journey Through Time Scenic Byway, began the last week of October, outside the small community of Escalante.

If you are an intrepid explorer, willing to hike and get your feet wet (and if you can negotiate slick rock and sandy washes), countless hidden patches of autumn are waiting for you. However, if you find easy walks and roadside viewing enough to satisfy your desire for adventure, as we do,

Highway 12 itself and the Burr Trail Road—and for a side trip, the Hole-in-the-Rock Road—will fill the bill nicely.

Lower Calf Creek Falls is a popular attraction. This impressive 126-foot waterfall drops down a colorful sandstone rock face. The trailhead to the falls is about halfway between the towns of Boulder and Escalante. The nearly 6-mile round-trip hike is a bit more than an easy walk, but the steep sections are short and without technical difficulty. The entire bottom of the canyon is filled with amber hues at this time of year. Cascading water in the desert is always a miracle.

From pullouts on the ridge high above the canyons of the Escalante River drainage, visitors can look down on these ribbons of fall color slicing their way through sheer rock. Just eight minutes by car from the waterfall, the Escalante River Trailhead leads to

POINTS of INTEREST

LENGTH
123 miles

REST STOP
Just off Highway 12, Boulder Mountain Lodge is a convenient place to stay. Plus, an 11-acre bird sanctuary surrounds the lodge. *boulder-utah.com*

SIDE TRIPS
Spot the Milky Way as it twinkles in the dark skies over Capitol Reef National Park. *nps.gov/care*

Hole-in-the-Rock Road is a 62-mile one-way route that follows a path taken by Mormon pioneers on their way to a new settlement in 1879. If you have a high-clearance vehicle with four-wheel drive, this is the place for off-roading.

When the settlers reached a thin crack in the canyon rim, they camped and worked all winter to widen the opening so 250 people, over 1,000 animals and 83 wagons could pass. The actual Hole in the Rock is at mile 55.

Devils Garden, about 12 miles down the road, is popular for its oddly shaped rock formations.

▼

Witness wildlife such as mule deer in Capitol Reef National Park.

a short, easy walk through lovely cottonwoods, and there is an overlook above the river on the south side.

Heading north from Escalante toward Capitol Reef National Park, we took a side trip along the Burr Trail Road outside the town of Boulder. The western part of the road is paved, and this 17-mile section of the Burr Trail is among our favorites in fall for two reasons: Long Canyon and the Gulch. Above both gorges, pullouts look out on phenomenal views of golden trees dwarfed by red canyon walls.

We ended our Highway 12 road trip with two nights in Torrey, on the edge of Capitol Reef National Park. Fall color is so close to park roads, it almost demands you to stop and admire it.

One of the best places for leaf peeping is just across the highway from the Capitol Reef National Park Visitor Center. Fantastic monumental natural sculptures of Navajo and Wingate sandstone rise up all around, dominated by one that's called the Castle. Cottonwoods in twos and threes follow the course of Sulphur Creek at the base of the formations as its waters flow to the junction with the Fremont River, carving a narrow route through the Waterpocket Fold, a 100-mile-long buckle in Earth's surface.

Autumn in this arid part of the West is unique. Here, unlike many places, you can see a handful of glowing cottonwoods softening the outlines of towering red rock formations. ◼

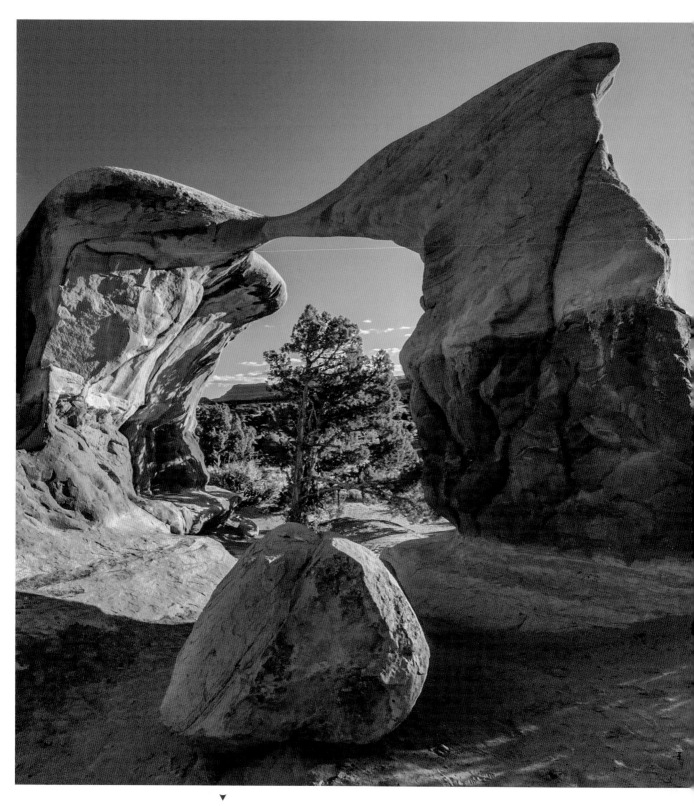

▼
Highway 12 leads to many wonders, including the rock arches of Devils Garden.

▼

Lupine blossom across the side of Steptoe Butte.

STORY BY **MARY LIZ AUSTIN**
PHOTOS BY **MARY LIZ**
AUSTIN & TERRY DONNELLY

HEART OF THE PALOUSE

WASHINGTON'S U.S. HIGHWAY 195 SERVES UP SOME OF THE WORLD'S MOST FERTILE AND UNIQUELY SCENIC FARMLAND.

IT'S A LATE AFTERNOON IN JUNE as Terry and I make a beeline down U.S. Highway 195 in the heart of Washington's Palouse country. Heavy rain clouds have accompanied us on our drive to the southeastern corner of our state, and it appears they might clear.

When you say "clearing storm" to photographers on the way to a shoot, watch them step on the gas.

The Palouse, one of the most productive agricultural regions in the world, encompasses thousands of square miles of undulating hills formed by wind-borne silt. As you drive through, you can't help but imagine you're at sea, with clusters of grain elevators and isolated barns resembling ships' hulls breaking against the sky.

Rivers and streams did not create these rolling hills; there are no continuous valleys in the area, and the hills don't connect. Rather, a series of geologic events forged the Palouse—massive floods, volcanic eruptions, lava flows and dust storms that blew silt from the South. Some say that at today's wind speeds it would take 25,000 years to re-create one 80-foot hill of silt.

U.S. Highway 195 runs from Spokane, Washington, to Lewiston, Idaho, just across the border. Along the way it passes through a number of friendly farm towns, as well as Pullman, home of Washington State University. My favorite section of the road spans Whitman County, a 55-mile stretch from Rosalia to Uniontown. I love to stay in the bustling town of Colfax. With roads radiating in all directions, it's a wonderful base camp for exploring the Palouse.

Head to Steptoe Butte State Park in the small town of Steptoe for the region's most dramatic view. The butte,

▼

The iron-wheel fence of Dahmen Barn.

POINTS of INTEREST

LENGTH
105 miles

FUN FACT
Frank Smith discovered a giant earthworm in the soil near Pullman in 1897. *Driloleirus americanus* can grow to be 3 feet long; it was last spotted in 2010.

SIDE TRIP
Palouse Falls is a must-see for anyone traveling through the area. The Palouse River drops 198 feet into a rocky canyon, making for one of the most beautiful landmarks in the state of Washington. *parks.wa.gov*

a towering thimble-shaped remnant of an ancient mountaintop, is easy to spot in this sea of green. A spiraling road leads to the 3,612-foot summit, and panoramic views of the outlying farmlands and towns appear as soon as you start the ascent. On a clear day you can see for 200 miles from the top. It's a perfect place to watch raptors ride the wind currents while sunlight rakes the patchwork fields—and on this day, to photograph a clearing storm!

There are also plenty of handsome barns in this region, built by early settlers to store hay, shelter farm animals and serve as workshops. Today, many have been remodeled to fill new roles. One of our favorites, the Dahmen Barn in Uniontown, once housed a commercial dairy operation. Now it's a thriving art center with studio space for 20 local artists and a very distinctive fence constructed from a thousand antique iron farm-machinery wheels. Resident artists teach classes in painting and other media to visitors of all ages.

I especially love this area in June, with its colorful mix of greens ranging from maturing wheat fields to the new fuzz of germinating legumes. In July, you will see golden waves of ripe wheat and bright yellow canola flowering against a blue sky as red barns peek out of the folds of the hills.

Of course, you can enjoy the view from 195 any time of year. The seasons transform the Palouse. In autumn, the changing leaves of deciduous trees add vibrant oranges, reds and yellows to the horizon. Farmers bring out their machinery to harvest crops, adding another layer of depth to the surrounding landscape. In winter, light snow drapes these rolling hills in serenity and stillness. Come spring, the cycle begins again, and beautifully blossoming wildflowers emerge on hillsides and buttes. Spring weather is unpredictable, with storms as sudden as they are intense.

You might even catch that clearing storm and see a cloud sailing across the sky with a rainbow for its tail! ◾

▼
A weathered barn stands before a carpet of ripe canola.

▼

Isolated farms look like ships in a sea of wheat throughout the Palouse.

" **Another glorious day,
the air as delicious to
the lungs as nectar
to the tongue."**

—JOHN MUIR

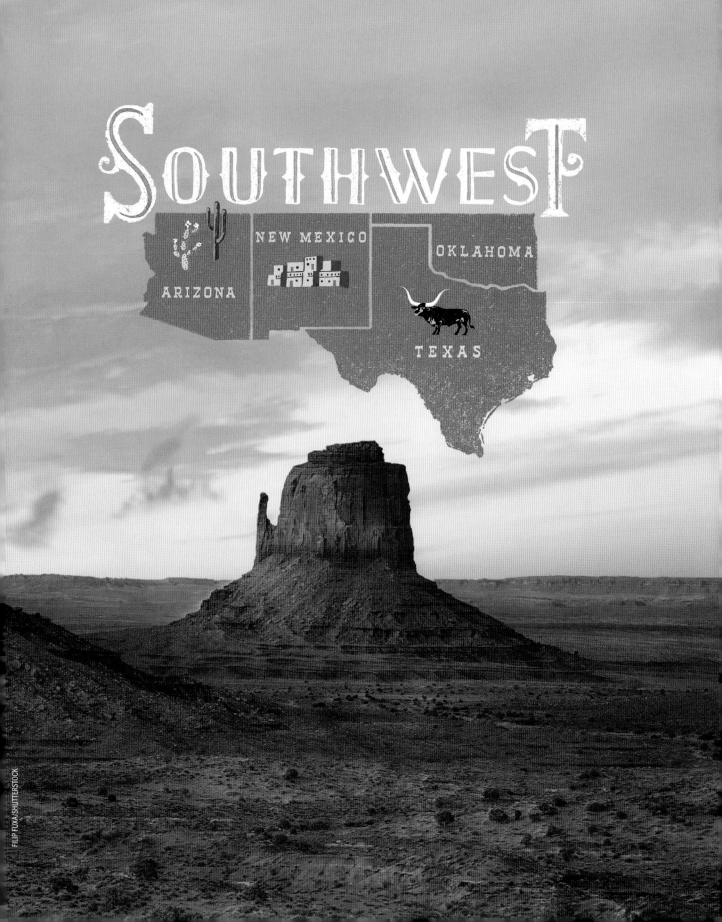

SOUTHWEST

ARIZONA

NEW MEXICO

OKLAHOMA

TEXAS

STORY BY **DONNA B. ULRICH**
PHOTOS BY **LARRY ULRICH**

APACHE TRAIL

MEET THE ROAD THAT MAKES RENTAL CAR DRIVERS WEEP.

THE APACHE TRAIL is not for the faint of heart who prefer their roads paved and with guardrails. Though the 41.5-mile drive snakes through some of the most beautiful and rugged terrain in the Sonoran Desert, it's a challenge for drivers unaccustomed to one-lane dirt roads with turnouts, precipitous drop-offs and nothing between you and the canyon below.

The first time we drove it, in the early '80s, it was as rough as any regularly maintained road can be. One of Larry's favorite sayings (and one that has gotten us in trouble more than I care to reveal) is, "The road is on the AAA map; it must be good."

Larry studies maps constantly (that's why we get in trouble so often) and wants to go somewhere because it sounds cool. I have to admit, he was right about the Apache Trail.

The road has threads of history running through it. Also known as State Route 88, it follows a path first used by the Salado Indians to traverse the Superstition Mountains. Later it became a stagecoach route connecting Phoenix to Globe, and finally a roadway to construct dams along the Salt River.

Be there at dawn to capture an iconic image of the Arizona landscape. The road runs east to west, perfect for taking photos in early-morning and late-afternoon light.

The Apache Trail begins in Apache Junction and heads east into the Old West. You'll pass places with names like Goldfield Ghost Town, Sweetheart Peak, Lost Dutchman State Park and Tortilla Flat. Prehistoric cultural sites are scattered throughout the area, but our favorite at the east end of the trail is Tonto National Monument, well-preserved cliff dwellings inhabited by the Salado people in the 13th, 14th and 15th centuries.

Fish Creek Hill starts the second half of the drive; this is the stretch that can make the city driver in a rental car nervous. The pavement ends and the dusty road becomes a steep series of twists and turns. The road hangs on the side of Fish Creek Canyon, which drains the Superstition Mountains.

If you're looking for grand views, great geology, reservoirs full of fish, lots of hiking trails and a year-round creek, head out of the city and take a day to explore this historic trail. ✒

POINTS of INTEREST

LENGTH
41.5 miles

WORDS TO THE WISE
Start with a full tank of gas and plenty of water. The speed limits are low, so the drive may take you longer than expected.

SIDE TRIPS
Lost Dutchman State Park offers campsites and nature trails. The 300-acre park derives its name from Jacob Waltz, a shadowy figure who—according to legend—discovered a rich gold mine during the late 1800s but never revealed its exact whereabouts. Over the years, at least 36 treasure seekers have died or disappeared seeking the elusive lode.

Tortilla Flat was once a stagecoach stop. This resurrected ghost town has a cafe, country store and a permanent population of six. But its weekend visitors, lured by souvenir shops, prickly-pear ice cream and the cool waters of Tortilla Creek, are far greater in number.

NEARBY ATTRACTION
Superstition Mountain Museum, Apache Junction

Top: The storied Superstition Mountains loom over saguaro cactuses and wildflowers. Bottom: A creek trickles through West Boulder Canyon, Tonto National Forest.

▼

The view from Monument Valley's North Window presents an otherworldly landscape.

STORY AND PHOTOS BY
TIM FITZHARRIS

MONUMENT VALLEY

MEANDER AMONG ARIZONA AND UTAH'S FAMOUS SPIRES,
PINNACLES AND BUTTES, WHICH ARE EVEN MORE AMAZING
IN REAL LIFE THAN THEY ARE IN THE MOVIES.

YOU'VE PROBABLY SEEN THIS PLACE before in a zillion cowboy movies, not to mention *Thelma & Louise, Forrest Gump* and Road Runner cartoons. Monument Valley, mostly in Arizona and partly in Utah, is every bit as impressive in real life.

For starters, it generates a feeling of the surreal, a combination of film deja vu and otherworldly landforms. I ask myself, *Am I really seeing this without a remote in my hand?* Well, it's there for sure, and you can drive among the soaring 400- to 1,000-foot red monoliths and scamper about jumbled boulders.

For photographers like me, it's an abundance of powerful graphic elements just waiting to be wrestled into a composition. The giant towers of rock, glowing red against a blue sky, have names to match their extravagant shapes: Totem Pole, Bear and Rabbit, Elephant Butte, the Mittens, Gray Whiskers and Rain God Mesa.

Monument Valley is Navajo Nation tribal land, and occasionally you'll see their herdsmen, wild ponies and livestock wandering through the mesas. I also look for these when I'm shooting photos, as they make great perspective

POINTS of INTEREST

LENGTH
17 miles

FUN FACT
In the mid-1500s, when Spanish explorers first encountered the southwestern Native American tribes, there were three major cultures in the Southwest: the Hohokam, an agricultural group located in the river valleys of the desert; the Mogollon, who were hunters and gatherers; and the Anasazi, who were cliff dwellers.

WORDS TO THE WISE
When on Indian reservations, abide by local customs. Ask permission before taking photos; never disturb artifacts.

SIDE TRIP
Directly east of Monument Valley find Four Corners Navajo Tribal Park. Here you can stand in the spot where Arizona, Utah, Colorado and New Mexico meet.

NEARBY ATTRACTIONS
Grand Canyon National Park, Arizona; Petrified Forest National Park, near Holbrook, Arizona; Zion National Park, Springdale, Utah

This aptly named oddity is Mushroom Rock.

references that show the grand scale of this place.

The 17-mile scenic drive through the valley features 11 numbered stops, each with a special view of rock formations. If you want to photograph the sand dunes like I did, you need to hire a Navajo guide to escort you into these areas. It's worth the extra fee. You don't need four-wheel drive, but a high-clearance vehicle saves wear and tear on your car.

The photographic challenge is timing the sun's route to spotlight rock faces and sandstone summits. I accomplish this by rising before dawn, and driving, hiking, rock-scrambling and chasing the perfect light and shadows by car during the day.

A spiritual place for the Navajo people, Monument Valley's exotic desert wilderness works its magic on most anyone. ❧

▼

As the sun rises behind East Mitten rock, it's clear how it received its name.

In autumn, sumacs, oaks and maples paint Oak Creek Canyon in gold and crimson.

Arizona

STORY BY
MARIJA ANDRIC

OAK CREEK CANYON

RED ROCKS, STEEP SWITCHBACKS AND DRAMATIC VIEWS MAKE THIS ARIZONA DRIVE A NAIL-BITER.

GROWING UP IN ARIZONA, I loved the biodiversity of the state. Minutes from my home, I could hike the best trails in the Sonoran Desert, and after a few hours of driving, I could breathe fresh alpine air and marvel at fall foliage. And there's one scenic drive in Arizona that has it all: Oak Creek Canyon.

This 15-mile state-designated scenic road along Route 89A begins in Sedona (if you're coming from Phoenix) and winds its way north to Flagstaff. It curves up the Colorado Plateau from the high desert to a landscape of ponderosa pines.

Getting to the start of the drive is a treat for the senses. Route 89A rolls through Oak Creek Village, passing iconic red rocks that are named for their shapes. The landscape has an unearthly feel, and its singular beauty is unforgettable. Bell Rock, which is just off the road, is a popular spot to pull over for pictures or go on a hike along the lower, easier trail.

My family and I took this drive in the summer to escape the dry desert heat and in the fall to see the foliage, which begins to turn in November. After crossing the Midgley Bridge, our first stop was Slide Rock State Park, a 43-acre historic apple farm that was at one time the Pendley homestead. Growing apples in the high desert sounds far-fetched, but Frank Pendley mastered an innovative irrigation technique in 1912 that allowed his orchards to thrive. In fact, today park officials still use the same technique to water the remaining heirloom trees.

Though the apple orchard is amazing, the main attraction is the park's namesake natural slide, which is a slippery chute of worn sandstone about 80 feet long and up to 4 feet wide. The waters of Oak Creek, which carved this canyon, are icy cold and refreshing. Children and adults alike squeal in delight as the water carries them down the slide into a pool.

Algae makes the rocks especially slippery, so it's important to wear water shoes. It's also important to look up and appreciate the canyon walls and

POINTS of INTEREST

LENGTH
15 miles

FUN FACT
The dramatic reds and oranges in the rocks of Sedona come from iron oxide, left from a post-glacial ocean that filled the Verde Valley.

WORDS TO THE WISE
A Red Rock Pass is required if you want to stop and park your car along the drive.

SIDE TRIP
Thousands of years before Hollywood discovered the red rocks of Sedona and the beauty of Oak Creek Canyon, the Sinagua called this place home. Though they moved on centuries ago, they left behind the Palatki and Honanki cliff dwellings. The sites are open to the public and overseen by Coconino National Forest staff. Call 928-282-3854 to reserve a tour spot.

NEARBY ATTRACTIONS
Lowell Observatory, Flagstaff; Tlaquepaque district, Sedona; Fort Verde State Historic Park, Camp Verde; Sharlot Hall Museum, Prescott; Smoki Museum, Prescott

▼

Red Rock Crossing, with its view of Cathedral Rock, is a must-see.

cliffs that surround the park. I've never been disappointed by that view.

Back on the highway, you could easily stay in your car to take in the sights, but along the road, a few picnic sites, campgrounds and overlooks, such as Banjo Bill and Halfway, are well worth exploring.

The farther you drive, the higher you climb. The air cools, and by the time you reach the West Fork Trail, ponderosa pines appear alongside oaks and junipers. The trail, one of the most popular in the area, follows the west fork of Oak Creek.

In fall, the trees are ablaze with reds, oranges and yellows. The canyon walls soar, and the sound of the moving water soothes. You'll step onto a paved trail that leads to a footbridge over the creek and Mayhew's Lodge, the ruins of an old guesthouse that burned down in 1980. At that point, your West Fork Trail adventure begins. The in-and-out hike is about 6 miles round trip.

The thrilling part of the drive begins at Pumphouse Wash. For the following 2 miles, the road curves into a series of switchbacks, each steeper than the last.

If you're lucky enough to be the passenger, you'll see some gorgeous

views of the canyon. (My mother always kept her head down during this part of the drive.) If you're the driver, well, you're probably looking at your knuckles and the road ahead.

Years ago, my husband-to-be and I went on this curvy drive. Though I knew where we were going, he insisted on using GPS. As the GPS attempted to chart the switchbacks, the fine pink line of the road turned into a blob.

It's a slow drive to the top, but when you get there, be sure to stop at the Oak Creek Vista. Take a look back at where you've been, and marvel at the wonder of it all. The elevation changes and the diverse ecosystems of the drive are laid out before you. It's a popular stop with visitors. The overlook is also home to a market offering Native American arts and crafts.

At this point, you're on the Colorado Plateau's southwestern edge. This is commonly referred to as the Mogollon Rim. The air up here is cooler and the forest is thick with pine trees.

The old lumber town of Flagstaff (home to the San Francisco Peaks, Northern Arizona University and Route 66) lies ahead. But that's a scenic drive for another day. ●

▼

Slide Rock State Park's natural slide is an oasis of fun.

New Mexico

STORY AND PHOTO BY
ADAM SCHALLAU

NEW MEXICO'S NORTH

TRAVEL HIGHWAY 64, AND YOU'LL SEE WHY THIS STATE
IS DUBBED THE LAND OF ENCHANTMENT.

WHEN YOU PLAN A TRIP across New Mexico, you may have visions of arid desert and long stretches of flat, desolate roads. But if you're driving on Highway 64 in the northern reaches of the state, what you find will surprise you.

From the town of Cimarron in the northeast, you leave the grasslands of the high plains behind and head west toward the Sangre de Cristo Mountains. Along the way, you'll follow the Cimarron River as it flows through Cimarron Canyon State Park, where tall cliffs known as the Palisades dominate the landscape.

As the road climbs up out of the canyon, you are rewarded with a view of the Moreno Valley. The valley is home to the towns of Eagle Nest and Angel Fire, which is where parts of the TV miniseries *Lonesome Dove* were filmed. This area is also part of the Enchanted Circle Scenic Byway, a great detour from Highway 64. The Sangres surround Moreno Valley. Wheeler Peak, the tallest in the state and part of the Sangres, sits at the northern end of the valley.

Continuing west, you will come to the historic town of Taos, which is known for its countless artists, adobe architecture, great northern New Mexican cuisine and the Taos Pueblo community. Be sure to give yourself plenty of time to explore the area as well as the many galleries and museums in Taos.

About 10 miles northwest of Taos, you'll cross Rio Grande Gorge Bridge 650 feet above the Rio Grande Gorge. The gorge, which is part of the Rio Grande del Norte National Monument, is the result of a separation in the Earth's crust as tectonic plates scraped against each other. A walk across the bridge is not for the faint of heart, but the view is stunning.

Next pass through the village of Tres Piedras. Here you'll discover that the forest is a mix of pines in the lower elevations, transitioning to aspens as you reach the high point on the journey at over 10,000 feet at Brazos Cliffs. When you look back on the experience, you can see why New Mexicans call their state The Land of Enchantment. ◾

POINTS of INTEREST

NOT TO BE MISSED
Every July, Native American dancers from across the country perform traditional dances at the Taos Pueblo Pow Wow. *taos.org/ events/taos-pueblo-pow-wow*

WORDS TO THE WISE
Roads can be icy and snowpacked in winter and early spring.

NEARBY ATTRACTIONS
Aztec Ruins National Monument, Aztec; Bisti Wilderness and Chaco Culture National Historical Park, south of Farmington; Heron Lake State Park, near Rutheron; Kit Carson Home and Museum, Taos

▼
Rio Grande River Gorge must have startled early explorers who happened upon it.

▼ *The Talimena Scenic Byway cuts through the Ouachita National Forest.*

STORY AND PHOTOS BY
INGE JOHNSSON

TALIMENA SCENIC BYWAY

GORGEOUS SCENERY GREETS YOU AT EVERY TURN ON THIS
SURPRISING TRIP IN SEARCH OF FALL COLOR IN OKLAHOMA.

YOU MAY NOT THINK OF OKLAHOMA as a place of natural splendor—especially not one with blazing fall colors. Yet the Sooner State has plenty of beautiful scenery. For the best fall leaf-peeping, grab the car keys and head to the Talimena Scenic Byway. The route is located in the large, dense Ouachita National Forest (pronounced WASH-i-tah), which crosses the state line between Oklahoma and Arkansas. Named after the towns on each end of the drive, the 54-mile byway stretches from Talihina, Oklahoma, to Mena, Arkansas.

Curving roads on the mountain ridge follow some of the highest peaks in the area, including Rich Mountain and Winding Stair Mountain. If you can resist stopping to marvel at the many vistas and attractions along the way, the route takes 1½ to two hours to drive. A leisurely trip can take all day

POINTS of INTEREST

LENGTH
54 miles

REST STOPS
Stay atop Rich Mountain, Arkansas' second-highest peak, at Queen Wilhelmina State Park Lodge, and relax on one of the inviting porches with panoramic views, or hike the nearby trails. *arkansasstate parks.com*

Step back in time to experience an old-fashioned home-style breakfast or lunch at the Skyline Cafe in Mena.

WORDS TO THE WISE
Bring your hiking boots, bicycle, ATV or horse to view the spectacular fall foliage from the trails in Talimena State Park, Oklahoma's entrance to the Talimena Scenic Byway. *travelok. com/talimena*

SIDE TRIP
Drive about an hour south of the byway to Beavers Bend State Park, where you can canoe on Broken Bow Lake, trout fish on Mountain Fork River, go biking, play a round of golf and more. *travelok.com/ beaversbend*

▼
Vibrant foliage lines the banks of Big Creek.

or more, but I recommend spending two to three days in the area to really take it all in.

There are many options for overnight accommodations, including camping, cabins, hotels and lodges. Pitch a tent at Winding Stair Campground, which has drive-up camping sites and a walk-in camp area for backpackers.

Talimena Scenic Byway is also a photographer's paradise. Twenty-two panoramic lookouts invite you to stop, explore and photograph the incredible views, steep inclines, fall foliage and abundant wildlife. The fiery red and gold fall colors in this area peak from mid-October to early November, depending on the weather, so let's go! ●

▼
Evening settles over Holson Valley Vista.

STORY AND PHOTO BY
LAURENCE PARENT

TEXAS HILL COUNTRY

RIVERS FLOW THROUGH CANYONS COVERED IN SEASONAL
GLORY ON THIS LONE STAR DRIVE.

I START MY 70-MILE DRIVE across the most rugged part of Texas Hill Country at the Medina River in Bandera. Tall bald cypresses arch over the clear water, their needles starting to show a rusty orange autumn hue.

Known for its rolling hills, rivers, lakes and spring wildflowers, Hill Country has plenty of scenic drives. But the route that starts in Bandera, the "cowboy capital of the world," is one of my favorites.

Texas Highway 16 moves past Bandera's quaint downtown. I follow the river upstream and soon arrive in the small town of Medina, known for its surrounding apple orchards.

Going west on RM 337 (the RM stands for ranch-to-market road), I climb out of the Medina River Valley, over a steep divide, and down to a junction with RM 187, which leads to a side trip to the Lost Maples State Natural Area in the town of Vanderpool.

Established to preserve the area's trees, rare plants and animals, Lost Maples is home to deeply incised canyons at the headwaters of the Sabinal River that offer shelter from the sun and wind, and a rare, isolated stand of bigtooth maples.

I admire splashes of gold and scarlet along the Maple Trail, one of several in the park. Heading up the East Trail to Hale Hollow, a narrow, rocky passage with ferns growing from the canyon wall and flaming maples spreading overhead, I breathe in the scent of turning leaves and then hike out over a ridge and head to my car.

Back on RM 337, views of multiple canyons open up from the highway. After only a few miles, the narrow road snakes its way down into another valley, this one cut by the bald cypress-lined West Sabinal River. Here, the vistas are never-ending, popping up with each bend in the road.

Soon the highway drops again into yet another valley and continues to Leakey, crossing the Frio River on the east side of the small town. I go south on U.S. 83 and end my drive at Garner State Park. The Frio River tumbles over boulders as it flows through the park. I park my car; the clear water beckons. ●

▼
The Sabinal River rolls past bigtooth maples and black cherry trees.

POINTS *of* INTEREST

LENGTH
70 miles

NOT TO BE MISSED
Fiesta San Antonio, San Antonio; Rodeo (summer), Bandera; Texas State Arts and Crafts Fair, Kerrville

FUN FACT
One of Texas's most enjoyable spectacles are the wildflowers that carpet its roadsides—the result of decades of planning. Beginning in the 1930s, the state harvested tons of seeds from donors and planted them along the highways (thus eliminating mowing expenses). In 1982 one of the program's most ardent champions, Lady Bird Johnson, founded a national wildflower research center in Austin.

SIDE TRIP
Medina earned its nickname as Texas' apple capital thanks to an abundance of orchards. Pick your own or find delicious apple products at Love Creek Orchards. *lovecreek orchards.com*

▼

Dawn breaks over a field of bluebonnets and Indian paintbrushes near Fredericksburg, Texas.

DEAN FIKAR/GETTY IMAGES

" **Where flowers bloom,
so does hope.**"

—LADY BIRD JOHNSON

MidWEST

NORTH DAKOTA

SOUTH DAKOTA

NEBRASKA

KANSAS

MINNESOTA

IOWA

MISSOURI

WISCONSIN

ILLINOIS

MICHIGAN

INDIANA

OHIO

▼
Maple leaves frame a gorgeous waterfall at Matthiessen State Park.

STORY AND PHOTOS BY
TERRY DONNELLY

ILLINOIS RIVER ROAD

SMALL TOWNS, PRETTY FARMS AND SURPRISING CLIFFS AND CANYONS DOT THIS SCENIC VALLEY.

OVER THE YEARS I'VE HEARD north-central Illinois—the place where I was born and raised—referred to in various ways. Flat as a pancake. America's heartland. A great place to raise a family. And, in fact, all of these observations are true.

The Illinois River Road National Scenic Byway provides a fine chance to come up with your own conclusions about this land, which is full of beautiful farms, hardwood forests, tallgrass prairies and unexpected geological surprises.

The reason I love to drive along this route today is not to engage the Illinois River itself as I once did, but to experience the profound and fascinating things the river has created.

You might be surprised by how flat the region actually is. Blame the glaciers; they scraped the Midwest smooth. But as the glaciers receded, they shed vast amounts of meltwater, which carved some of the world's most bucolic river valleys and dramatic sandstone canyons. The Illinois River is one such watershed: it drains waters from the Lake Michigan region into the Mississippi River.

Ottawa, the seat of LaSalle County, is a great place to start this drive. It is less than two hours southwest of Chicago and the site of the first Lincoln-Douglas debate in 1858. Check out the seasonal Saturday farmers market and the Old Town District.

From Ottawa, drive south across the river and follow its southern banks along Illinois Route 71 to Starved Rock, the gemstone of Illinois' state parks. The park's name is a homage to a tragic legend about a vengeful war between the Illini tribe on one side, and the Ottawa and Potawatomi on the other.

The besieged Illini took their final refuge by climbing the cliffs of a butte on the river. And with their enemies blocking access to food and water, the Illini starved there. Today Starved Rock draws outdoor enthusiasts with miles of hiking trails woven along scenic sandstone cliffs, wooded canyons with spring wildflowers, quiet streams, and waterfalls that flow heavily in spring and freeze over in winter for ice

Native wildflowers bloom in a prairie at Starved Rock State Park.

POINTS of INTEREST

LENGTH
291 miles

FUN FACTS
Traveling the country roads will surprise you with a village every 8 or 10 miles. These spots may support a gas station, grocery store or a restaurant. Places like Ladd, Cherry, Tiskilwa, Neponset, Bureau Junction, Zearing and Troy Grove have a fascinating history— usually of coal mining, or maybe a grain elevator on the railroad tracks.

NEARBY ATTRACTIONS
Owen Lovejoy Homestead, Princeton; Hegeler Carus Mansion, LaSalle

climbing. There are open tallgrass prairies that bloom in August and, of course, there's the river.

Adjacent to Starved Rock, west on Route 71, is smaller but equally engaging Matthiessen State Park. A quiet place of natural beauty, its features include deep sandstone dells, streams and waterfalls carved into the wooded terrain. It was once a private estate that was donated to the state.

To the north, and across the river from both of these parks, is the hamlet of North Utica with an assortment of family-owned shops and restaurants.

Westward along U.S. Route 6 from North Utica, the next cities to see are individual but are collectively known as LaSalle-Peru. These closely linked communities also encompass the cities of Oglesby and Spring Valley. These towns are known for classic architecture and brick downtowns.

LaSalle's commercial district is on the National Register of Historic Places. This is small-town America at its best. Many restaurants here are inspired by the culture of supper clubs.

Back on the road, a perfectly good interstate highway, I-80, goes straight through the Illinois Valley. Avoid it.

The countryside in LaSalle, Bureau and Putnam counties is the reason you are on this drive. These rural blacktop roads take you on a tour through some of the best farmland in America: corn and soybean country.

Winding westward along U.S. Route 6, you get to Princeton, the county seat of Bureau County and hub of agricultural commerce. It's steeped in history.

Here brick streets crisscross neighborhoods with elegant homes claiming carriage houses and barns. The city is also home to one of Illinois' five remaining covered bridges. From Princeton, heading south along Illinois Route 29 brings you once again beside the Illinois River and its wildlife.

There's quite a bit to explore, much to see and do, and great people to meet along the Illinois River Road. ●

Autumn means pumpkin season at Miller's Market in Neponset.

▼

Colorful leaves drape over the winding road into Copper Harbor.

STORY AND PHOTOS BY
CHUCK HANEY

KEWEENAW PENINSULA

MAKE YOUR WAY THROUGH LUSH FORESTS, GHOST TOWNS AND
COPPER MINES ON MICHIGAN'S HIGHWAY 41.

EXPLORING THE SCENIC KEWEENAW located in Michigan's Upper Peninsula is especially glorious in autumn, when the hardwood forests of sugar maples, birch, basswood and ash turn vibrant shades of red, yellow and gold along meandering U.S. Highway 41.

My favorite section of the enchanting highway is the 46-mile stretch from the twin cities of Houghton and Hancock northeast to Copper Harbor, where the mighty blue waters of Lake Superior lap against the coastal village. On the last few miles into Copper Harbor, a spectacular canopy of hardwood trees forms a tunnel along the Keweenaw's twists and turns. It's sheer driving bliss for leaf peepers!

The journey begins on the Portage Lake Lift Bridge, which connects Houghton and Hancock. It's the world's heaviest and widest double-decked lift bridge, with its center section designed to rise 100 feet to permit ships to pass through the canal. Here the Keweenaw Peninsula becomes a narrow island.

Nearby are remnants of the once-thriving copper mining industry. You can even take an underground tour of the huge Quincy Mine just north of Hancock from May to October. A cogwheel tram takes visitors to an area where they can explore the 2,400-foot section of the seventh level.

My next stop along the route is my favorite, the town of Calumet. I love wandering the brick streets to check out the architecture in the Old Red Jacket Downtown Historic District (the town was originally called Red Jacket). Especially endearing is the Calumet Theatre, which first opened its doors in 1900 and is still in use, with more than 60 shows booked annually and 700 seats for its patrons.

Visitors can learn about the peninsula's history at Coppertown USA, a mining museum on Calumet's Red Jacket Road. Railroad items include a four-man, gas-driven rail car and a Russell locomotive with a snowplow nearly as tall as a house.

You can then cross Highway 41 to the small town of Laurium to tour the Laurium Manor Inn (tour times are limited, so call ahead). The stately

Historic Eagle Harbor Lighthouse looks out over Lake Superior.

POINTS of INTEREST

LENGTH
46 miles

FUN FACTS
In the ghost town of Gay, half an hour east of Laurium, are ruins of the Mohawk Mining Co., opened in 1898. By 1932, residual sand from the method of separating copper and ore went a mile beyond the original shore. Boaters still use a 265-foot smokestack as a landmark.

Upper Michigan mines produced a majority of the United States' copper from 1845 to '77.

At least 27 scenic waterfalls can be enjoyed on the Keweenaw Peninsula.

NEARBY ATTRACTIONS
Eagle Harbor Lighthouse, Eagle Harbor; Eagle Harbor Lifesaving Station and Museum, Eagle Harbor

13,000-square-foot mansion is the largest and likely the most opulent of the homes built on the peninsula by wealthy copper mine owners. For those who want to stay in the 45-room mansion, now a bed-and-breakfast, there are 10 guest rooms, all with private baths.

Scattered along Highway 41 are small ghost towns that thrived during the copper mining heyday as well as country churches and general stores. Shops offer a local favorite called a pasty, a baked pastry filled with vegetables and meat and topped with gravy. You'll become an honorary "Yooper" (UP-er) after a few of these meat pies, which filled the immigrant Cornish and Finnish miners' bellies after a long day of scraping for copper.

Among the ghost towns is Delaware, where you can take a self-guided tour through the Delaware Mine, one of the oldest on the peninsula.

I like to take a walk along a lovely forested trail leading to the ghost town of Mandan, where 300 residents once thrived in the mining days.

The ghost town of Phoenix has the restored historic Church of the Assumption, which features a white steeple that has been stoically pointing toward the heavens since 1899.

Once in Copper Harbor, I shake off the road weariness by mountain biking along the superb trail system built by the town's adventure-seeking residents or by paddling away in a sea kayak in Lake Medora.

For grander adventure, I can strike out with friends on Lake Superior and take in rocky sea stacks and stately lighthouses. History buffs may want to explore the well-preserved buildings and equipment at Fort Wilkins Historic Complex and State Park.

One jaunt that is immensely worthwhile is the picturesque drive to scenic Brockway Mountain, where the gorgeous views of vast Lake Superior from the northern tip of the peninsula are always awe-inspiring.

To end your Keweenaw exploration, take in the sunset and enjoy a dinner of locally caught whitefish while reflecting on the day's adventure. ✺

▼
Portage Lake Lift Bridge connects the cities of Hancock and Houghton.

▼ *Sleeping Bear Dunes National Lakeshore hugs the northeast shore of Lake Michigan.*

STORY AND PHOTOS BY
MARY LIZ AUSTIN

LEELANAU PENINSULA

MICHIGAN'S M-22 TRAVELS THROUGH GREAT LAKES SCENERY WITH LIGHTHOUSES, QUAINT VILLAGES AND HISTORIC FARMS.

IT'S SHORTLY AFTER SUNRISE when I settle into a cafe booth in the tiny town of Empire, Michigan. The waitress pours coffee with one hand as she points to the menu board with the other.

After a quick scan, I'm stumped on one of the items: two eggs with scrapple and hash browns. "What's scrapple?" I ask.

"Oh," the waitress replies, "it has a variety of things, but you probably don't want to know what they are. Let's just say it's similar to hash. It's good, and very popular. Trust me."

The crisp October air has given me the appetite of a lumberjack, so I decide to trust her and give it a try.

I am working my way along M-22, a Michigan Heritage Route that follows about 100 miles of Lake Michigan shoreline on the scenic Leelanau Peninsula. (On a map of lower Michigan, it's where your left little finger would be in the mitten.)

Like scrapple, this drive also has a variety of things, but these are things you really do want to know

about. A rich and varied history and landscape make this a something-for-everyone type of place. You can find an abundance of beaches, lakes and rivers, in addition to historic farming communities and quaint villages from the area's lumbering days.

Lighthouse hunters will enjoy two favorites anchoring each end of M-22. On the southern end, a complete rehab has restored Point Betsie Lighthouse to its historic World War II state. The Grand Traverse Lighthouse in Leelanau State Park guards the peninsula's northern tip.

In between, Sleeping Bear Dunes National Lakeshore offers a vast number of interesting things to explore. For dramatic vistas, Pierce Stocking Scenic Drive is a 7.4-mile loop with spectacular overlooks of the Glen Lakes, Lake Michigan and the extensive Sleeping Bear dune system.

The National Park Service, private organizations and individual owners have preserved more than 300 historic rural structures in this area. One of my

▼

A maple tree in fall splendor in the Port Oneida Rural Historic District.

POINTS of INTEREST

LENGTH
About 100 miles

NOT TO BE MISSED
The National Cherry Festival, Traverse City

FUN FACT
With its abundant orchards, award-winning wineries and fine swimming beaches, Leelanau lives up to its name, a Chippewa word meaning "delight of life."

NEARBY ATTRACTIONS
Colonial Michilimackinac, a reconstructed fur-trading village, Mackinaw City; Mackinac Island, "the Bermuda of the North," accessible by ferry from St. Ignace and Mackinaw City

favorites is the D.H. Day farmstead, which includes one of the nation's most-photographed barns. This magnificent white structure, with towering twin silos flanking its main door, dates back to the late 1800s.

North of Sleeping Bear Dunes is the port town of Leland, home to historic Fishtown and the ferry terminal for the Manitou Islands. Fishtown is a charming collection of weathered fishing shanties, smokehouses and shops along the Leland River. Working fish tugs and charter fishing boats that maintain the long tradition of Great Lakes maritime industry and culture are moored along this rustic quay.

Past Leland, the landscape unfolds in rolling hills with orchards, vineyards and wineries. The seasonal bounty of a produce stand lures me in. I'm greeted by roving hens and friendly golden retrievers and rewarded with apples, pumpkins, homemade preserves and pickled vegetables.

Continuing on past the village of Northport, the scenic route bends back to the southeast along the Grand Traverse Bay and ultimately reaches its end in Traverse City.

If you have an appetite for adventure, I recommend both the scrapple and M-22. Each you can sink your teeth into and come away satisfied. ◗

▼
The charming Point Betsie Lighthouse at dusk in Frankfort.

STORY BY
DARRYL R. BEERS

U.S. HIGHWAY 2

SANDY BEACHES AND AUTUMN BEAUTY AWAIT IN MICHIGAN'S
UPPER PENINSULA.

LIKE A KID CELEBRATING BIRTHDAYS, I never tire of traveling U.S. Highway 2 across Michigan's Upper Peninsula. For about 300 miles, the drive reveals a stunning array of landscapes—both natural and man-made. I always look forward to it.

Going from west to east, this drive starts in Ironwood and ends in my hometown of St. Ignace. Six hours of drive time will get you from one end to the other, but I highly recommend taking it slowly and breaking up the drive into two days.

The journey from Ironwood to Escanaba goes through a mostly forested stretch famous for its outstanding fall colors. The road winds through a large segment of Ottawa National Forest. Long stretches of highway have few man-made intrusions, and your eyes can feast on the brilliant hues of autumn.

About an hour into the drive, I take a 20-mile detour north to Bond Falls. Bond is one of the most spectacular falls in all of Michigan. The middle branch of the Ontonagon River flows through a series of small drops before

reaching the grand finale—a stunning 50-foot waterfall. A boardwalk allows visitors access to views from any angle.

After the detour, pick up the route again in Watersmeet. A few miles south of the town of Crystal Falls, the highway dips into Wisconsin for about 15 miles and twice crosses the Menominee River. On this stretch I once had to stop my car as a black bear sow and her two cubs ambled across the roadway—not an unusual sight.

Upon reaching Escanaba, explore Sand Point Lighthouse, faithfully restored to its original 1867 design, on the shore of Little Bay de Noc.

Much of the drive from Escanaba to St. Ignace borders Lake Michigan. Stretches of highway afford views of sandy beaches that seem endless. As you get closer to St. Ignace, roadside parks and overlooks offer looks of Lake Michigan and the Mackinac Bridge.

I spent one of my favorite moments on the entire U.S. 2 drive at one of these parks, watching a blazing orange sun slowly set over the still blue waters. Who knows how you'll be rewarded? ◗

▼

Summer wildflowers bloom on the shore of Lake Michigan.

POINTS of INTEREST

LENGTH
About 300 miles

SIDE TRIPS
At Palms Book State Park, at a 40-foot-deep natural spring known as Kitch-iti-kipi (the Indians called it "Mirror of Heaven"), you can board a wooden raft and, using a guide cord, pull yourself across the 200-foot-wide pond. The raft has windows that allow you to look into the depths at trout and limestone-coated fallen trees. The underground aquifer below maintains the water at a constant 45 degrees F.

At nearby Indian Lake State Park, an 8,400-acre body of water was named for the Indians who lived there more than a century ago. Today its pristine beaches attract swimmers and sunbathers, and its whitecapped waters are a lure for anglers.

After rejoining Route 2, head east into Manistique and cross the Siphon Bridge. Designed to float like the hull of a boat, at one time this remarkable road was 4 feet below the surface level of the Manistique River.

The sun's rays reflect off rocks in Lake Superior near the city of Grand Marais.

STORY AND PHOTOS BY
BOB FIRTH

NORTH SHORE SCENIC DRIVE

DISCOVER THE ALLURE OF MINNESOTA'S WILD SIDE BY CRUISING ALONG THE COAST OF LAKE SUPERIOR.

LAKE SUPERIOR'S NORTH SHORE is full of rugged rock, rivers, inland lakes and beautiful waterfalls. Many people think everything north of the Great Lakes is in Canada, but Minnesota has a nearly 145-mile-long "trail" running along Lake Superior from Duluth to Grand Portage, just miles shy of the border.

Even though it's really Highway 61, I call North Shore Scenic Drive a trail because it makes me feel as if I've gone back in time to the 1600s, when French explorers canoed and hiked here. Much of the land is still wild and unspoiled.

A moody Lake Superior shifts from peaceful sunrises and sunsets to thunderous storms that crash large waves against the rocky shore. In the winter, the lake transforms into an arctic-like landscape of frozen ice sculptures and caves.

People of all abilities can drive, bike, kayak and camp along the coast, explore by motorboat, or hike. The Superior Hiking Trail and Lake Superior State Water Trail draw nature lovers from around the world.

As you start your journey, pay a visit to the Duluth Ship Canal—it's the gateway to Duluth Harbor from Lake Superior for international ships. Standing out on the pier and witnessing

▼

Split Rock Lighthouse sits on a cliff south of Silver Bay.

POINTS of INTEREST

LENGTH
About 145 miles

NOT TO BE MISSED
The North Shore Fall Color Tour is accessible to anyone who doesn't mind gravel roads. Wind through woodlands of aspen and birch and explore the rolling hills of the Superior National Forest.

WORDS TO THE WISE
Since Route 61 is a busy highway, leave plenty of time for your trip.

NEARBY ATTRACTION
The Depot, an 1892 landmark train station that houses museums and performing arts organizations, Duluth

these enormous boats pass through the harbor is fascinating, as is watching the historic lift bridge in action.

My children enjoy walking the lichen-covered pathway to the Grand Marais Lighthouse while watching kayakers and bigger seaworthy vessels.

The shoreline offers endless beaches scattered with agates and driftwood. Beachcombing has always been one of my family's favorite pastimes. Several state parks, including Tettegouche,

Cascade River and Temperance River, offer access to these natural wonders.

Moving inland, you'll find a multitude of serene lakes, tumbling rivers and endless woodlands. I love to discover hidden waterfalls, and occasionally I encounter loons, moose, black bears and wolves.

Minnesota's North Shore is a place to find your own path and travel at your own pace. The entire trip is truly the destination. ✦

The Devil Track River attracts trout anglers, hikers and ice climbers.

This maple tree hangs over a horse and buggy on Ohio Route 643.

STORY AND PHOTOS BY
DOYLE YODER

OHIO'S AMISH COUNTRY

WANDER THROUGH A TAPESTRY OF CRESTING HILLS, DISTANT FORESTS AND LOVINGLY KEPT AMISH FARMSTEADS.

I GREW UP IN EASTERN OHIO AMISH COUNTRY, and I chose to make my life and my living here as a photographer. As far as I'm concerned, the roads that wind through the hills and valleys of Holmes, Coshocton, Tuscarawas and Wayne counties are some of the most inspiring scenic drives in America.

I'd be really hard-pressed to pick one favorite road. State Route 39 from Mansfield to Dover is perhaps the most popular one. It runs through beautiful rolling countryside and classic small towns such as Millersburg, Berlin,

Walnut Creek and Sugarcreek, "The Little Switzerland of Ohio."

But to truly appreciate the region's unique blend of scenery and culture, I encourage you to wander off on some of the smaller side roads. State Route 643, for example, runs from the Sugarcreek area southwest toward Coshocton, through the heart of some of the most unforgettable scenes in Amish country.

With birds chirping and a cool morning breeze in my face, life's simple pleasures unfold with each

POINTS of INTEREST

NOT TO BE MISSED
Ohio Swiss Festival, Sugarcreek

FUN FACT
With the approach of the bicentennial in 1976, Americans became very interested in their past and in the process discovered the unique art of Amish quilting. Because many of the Amish women spend time gardening and helping with the farming during the warmer months, they spend most of the winter sewing.

WORDS TO THE WISE
Beware of slow-moving horse-drawn buggies. Refrain from photographing the Amish.

NEARBY ATTRACTIONS
Canton Classic Car Museum and Pro Football Hall of Fame, Canton

▼
Colorful quilts dry on the line on a sunny afternoon.

passing mile. The view is a constantly changing tapestry of cresting hills, distant forests and lovingly kept Amish farmsteads. Each season brings its unique rewards.

In the spring, teams of magnificent draft horses are out plowing and planting in the fields, while Amish children play joyous games of baseball at recess. In summer, shocks of wheat and oats dry in eye-catching patterns and flowers bloom in well-tended gardens. In the fall, dew glistens off crisp corn shocks while sugar maples along the road burst into awesome color. Winter snows blanket field and forest in pristine white.

People often ask how I create such wonderful pictures. And while I'm always striving to master my trade, I can only reply that the most beautiful pictures I take will never match the beauty God has created here in this blessed little corner of Ohio. ✺

▼

A rainbow peeks from the clouds above a farm in Coshocton County.

The Sturgeon Bay Ship Canal Pierhead Lighthouse was constructed in 1881.

STORY BY
DARRYL R. BEERS

DOOR COUNTY COASTAL BYWAY

WISCONSIN HIGHWAY 42'S SMORGASBORD INCLUDES
VINEYARDS, HARBOR VILLAGES, PARK RETREATS AND
STUNNING BAYSIDE SUNSETS.

OVER THE COURSE OF SEVERAL DECADES spent exploring country roads, I find that none is more enjoyable than the 40-mile stretch of Wisconsin State Highway 42 going through northern Door County.

The adventure begins at Bayview Bridge, rising to a height of more than 50 feet above the Sturgeon Bay Ship Canal. The view on a sunny day is stunning—and endless—as the clear blue water stretches toward the waters of Green Bay to the west and Lake Michigan to the east. In any season you may see a massive 1,000-foot Great Lakes freighter sailing into Sturgeon Bay for repairs.

The next 15 miles north is mostly rural, with a sprinkling of markets, vineyards and specialty shops. Take time to stop and search for antiques or to enjoy a cup of gourmet coffee and culinary delights, many of which are unique to Door County.

Countryside suddenly gives way to bayside as Highway 42 veers into quaint Egg Harbor. This is the first of a handful of small, distinctive villages dotting the shoreline of Green Bay. When these lands were first settled, mostly in the mid-1800s, a safe harbor was necessary for survival. Today these harbors serve as a picturesque

POINTS of INTEREST

LENGTH
40 miles

NOT TO BE MISSED
The Door County "fish boil," an outdoor tradition featured at many restaurants

WORDS TO THE WISE
Reservations for lodging are recommended, especially from June to October. Those without reservations may inquire at the 24-hour Destination Door County Welcome Center, located at routes 57 and 42 at the southern edge of Sturgeon Bay.

NEARBY ATTRACTION
Green Bay Packers Hall of Fame, Green Bay

▼

A purple sky sets the scene while sailing at twilight on Green Bay.

backdrop for swimming, boating, fishing and sightseeing. Each locale offers stunning sunsets that color the bay's long horizon. Village streets are lined with unique shops, art galleries, fine eateries, confectioneries and more.

Cherry and apple orchards border many of the roadways between villages, serving up a visual feast of blossoms in the spring. At both Fish Creek and Ephraim, the highway affords direct access to Peninsula State Park, the

crown jewel of Wisconsin's park system. Peninsula State Park encompasses 3,776 acres of forests, meadows, wetlands and towering cliffs, as well as 8 miles of shoreline.

Highway 42's final 1.5 miles zig and zag through a beautiful maple and beech forest, ending at the Northport Ferry dock. Take the half-hour ferry ride to Washington Island or turn around and head back. Either way, I guarantee you'll enjoy the trip. ❧

▼
An early morning view of Lake Michigan from Cave Point County Park.

STORY AND PHOTOS BY
BOB FIRTH

GREAT RIVER ROAD

CHART A COURSE BESIDE THE UPPER MISSISSIPPI RIVER TO
SEE MAJESTIC BLUFFS AND TO VISIT CHARMING TOWNS.

ALONG A 150-MILE SPAN of the Upper Mississippi River from Red Wing, Minnesota, to Prairie du Chien, Wisconsin, the Great River Road National Scenic Byway offers beautiful vistas, quaint towns, history and culture, woodland hikes and many other hidden gems.

Without stops or detours, the trip can be completed in a few hours. But I recommend devoting a full day or two and seeing as much as possible.

My favorite tour of river country takes the Great River Road, mainly following U.S. Highway 61 in Minnesota and State Trunk Highway 35 located in Wisconsin. I look for side routes rising from the river's edge through steep woodlands, canyons and ravines. From the upper bluffs, the views of creeks, forests and farms are breathtaking.

Start in Red Wing, fueling up at Hanisch Bakery and Coffee Shop—one of Minnesota's best—and shop at Red Wing Shoe Store & Museum and Red Wing Stoneware & Pottery.

Then head toward Wabasha, Minnesota, to learn about eagles at the National Eagle Center. Cross the Wabasha-Nelson Bridge to see eagles in the wild and some great views of Mississippi River backwaters.

In the small town of Nelson, Wisconsin, grab a tasty bite to eat at J&J Barbecue or the Nelson Cheese Factory. Fountain City, Wisconsin, has a historic downtown, with entertaining stops close by at Elmer's Auto & Toy Museum and the funky Prairie Moon Sculpture Garden and Museum.

Winona, Minnesota, is known for its grand old banks, homes and churches. For super scenery, take some time to hike in Great River Bluffs State Park.

Near La Crosse, Wisconsin, big views of the Mississippi Valley are easily accessible with just a short walk. Check out Goose Island County Park and Grandad Bluff Park.

Farther south, find more stunning vistas at Pikes Peak State Park in McGregor, Iowa, and Wyalusing State Park near Prairie du Chien, Wisconsin.

Let the inspiring sights and sounds of the mighty Mississippi guide you on your way as you explore! ❧

POINTS of INTEREST

LENGTH
About 150 miles

NOT TO BE MISSED
Riverboat excursions from several cities, including La Crosse and Prairie du Chien in Wisconsin, and Dubuque in Iowa

FUN FACT
In fall, monarch butterflies and birds flock to Trempealeau National Wildlife Refuge in Wisconsin before they fly south. *fws.gov/refuge/ trempealeau*

NEARBY ATTRACTIONS
National Mississippi River Musuem & Aquarium, Dubuque, Iowa; *Field of Dreams* baseball diamond, setting for the motion picture, Dyersville, Iowa; Mall of America, the country's largest shopping mall, Bloomington, Minnesota

Top: Fall foliage frames a red barn in Frontenac, Minnesota. Bottom: A great blue heron fishes on the Mississippi River.

▼

The golden hues of autumn saturate the Minnesota banks of the Mississippi River.

7MICHAEL/GETTY IMAGES

" *In wildness is the preservation of the world.* "

—HENRY DAVID THOREAU

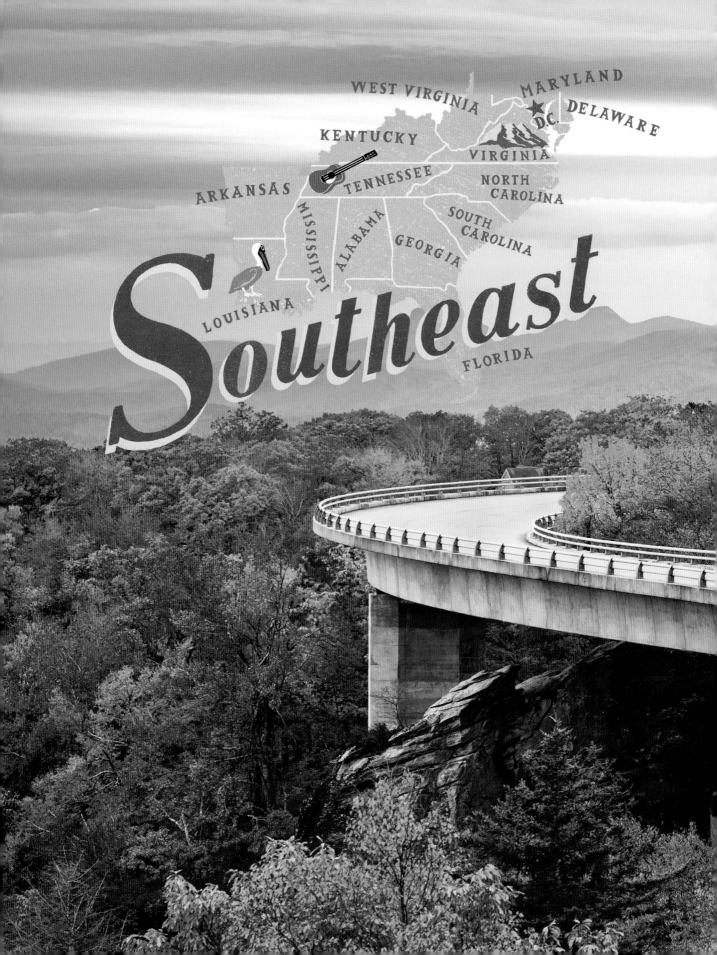

WEST VIRGINIA

MARYLAND

D.C. DELAWARE

KENTUCKY

VIRGINIA

ARKANSAS

TENNESSEE

NORTH CAROLINA

MISSISSIPPI

ALABAMA

SOUTH CAROLINA

GEORGIA

LOUISIANA

Southeast

FLORIDA

▼
The setting sun casts a majestic glow over Sam's Throne Recreation Area.

STORY AND PHOTOS BY
PAUL CALDWELL

SCENIC HIGHWAY 7

ARKANSAS' MOST BEAUTIFUL BYWAY CLIMBS INTO THE OZARK
MOUNTAINS, SHOWING OFF BLUFFS, CANYONS AND VALLEYS
AROUND EVERY CURVE.

ARKANSAS HAS MANY WONDERFUL state highways to explore, but Highway 7 is considered one of the most enthralling drives in America.

There are several places to pull over to enjoy a picturesque view, and plenty of side trips to take. My favorite drive along Highway 7 starts in Russellville and crosses the Arkansas River Valley going north before it climbs up into the Ozark Mountains.

The route stays high on the ridges until its long drop down into the charming mountain town of Jasper, so you can slow down, relax and soak up the scenery.

During the drive, make sure to look for wildlife. It's common to see herds of deer along the road, but if you get an early start, you may see a red fox, bobcat or even a black bear. Also keep your eyes on the power lines to look for the many species of hawks that frequent this part of the state.

Stop along Highway 7 at the scenic Rotary Ann Overlook. It's a treat to look due west at this vast vista and see into the heart of the Ozark Mountains.

About halfway between Russellville and Jasper, you'll encounter Sand Gap, formerly known as Pelsor. From there, you can consider two intriguing short side trips.

Highway 123 leads west to Haw Creek Falls, an impressive waterfall nestled in a mature hardwood forest. Highway 16 takes you east to Pedestal Rocks Scenic Area, a high bluff eroded into huge pedestals in lots of interesting shapes and sizes.

North of here you can make another short side trip to visit Sam's Throne Recreation Area, a long bluff line that wraps around the Big Creek valley. It's an easy hike to another stunning view of autumn colors at their peak. There is a campground here, so you can spend the night and rest up before continuing on your drive.

All along Highway 7, you'll notice lovely old barns and homes. Many of these rustic structures are located on

POINTS of INTEREST

LENGTH
290 miles

WORDS TO THE WISE
Steep grades make some roads off-limits to RVs.

SIDE TRIPS
Sam's Throne is a popular rock climbing destination with multiple paths for all experience and ability levels. It also draws hikers and tent campers.

Once you reach Jasper, look for the junction with Highway 74. Turn onto this road to reach the Buffalo National River. Two of the most popular areas to visit along this river are Ponca, home to herds of elk, and the Steel Creek Recreation Area and Campground. If you have extra time, consider renting a canoe for a float trip to view stone bluffs that stand more than 400 feet tall.

NEARBY ATTRACTIONS
Little Rock, the state capital; Eureka Springs, a mountainside resort community; Ozark Folk Center State Park, Mountain View

▼

Haw Creek Falls, near Sand Gap, is majestic in springtime.

national forest land, and you can pull off the highway to get some great pictures. Also look for antique cars and trucks; sometimes they're all that's left of the old homesites.

One of my favorite vantage points from high on the Ozark Mountain ridges is the view from the western rim of the Arkansas Grand Canyon.

For early risers, it's the perfect place to catch a sunrise. If you wish to explore this area in more depth, reserve a room at the Cliff House Inn, located 6 miles south of Jasper. The hotel offers wonderful views of the canyon, and its delicious morning breakfast menu is an added incentive to stay the night.

Once you're on the road again, look for the junction with Highway 374, just before the road drops into Jasper. This detour descends right into the Arkansas Grand Canyon and offers many intimate views of the area's lesser-seen beauty.

Arkansas' Scenic Highway 7 is an incredible drive through America's heartland in every season. ✿

▼
Erosion has left behind impressive formations at Pedestal Rocks.

STORY AND PHOTO BY
MARK LAGRANGE

BAYOU COUNTRY

THE ROMANCE AND HISTORY OF SOUTHERN LOUISIANA ARE REVEALED ALONG THE SOUTH'S OLD SPANISH TRAIL.

CHOOSING ASSORTED INGREDIENTS for a good gumbo is a fine parallel to meandering along the beautiful, uncommon traces of southern Louisiana. A journey through bayou country, which is steeped in Cajun French culture, isn't a traditional road trip. Although Highway 90, once known as the Old Spanish Trail, is the main route, it's the side roads that lead to places with a Southern culture all their own.

As you make your way westward on Highway 90 across southern Louisiana, the influence of the Atchafalaya River Basin on the surrounding landscape becomes evident. It is the largest intact river swamp in the U.S. and holds some of Louisiana's most scenic views. The basin, which stretches into the Gulf of Mexico, is a National Heritage Area.

From Highway 90, take Louisiana 329 to Avery Island, one of five salt domes that have moved the land above them to form "islands" within the marsh. Avery is also known as the birthplace of Tabasco pepper sauce. Take the Tabasco factory tour, and then spend time at the island's Jungle Gardens. The 170-acre preserve is dotted with blooming azaleas and camellias when in season. During warmer months, alligators sometimes sunbathe on the edge of several ponds throughout the gardens. Springtime offers a fabulous view of the thousands of egrets nesting in Bird City, the island's private pond.

Just north of Avery Island, the salt domes push up out of the swamp to form Jefferson Island, where you'll find the Joseph Jefferson Mansion. Built in the 1800s, the mansion boasts elegance and grandeur. The great oaks that surround it have stood for nearly 350 years.

No tour would be complete without a sampling of Louisiana's preserved Cajun French culinary culture. It's worth the time to stop in Breaux Bridge, which the state Legislature proclaimed the crawfish capital of the world. Visit during the famous Crawfish Festival the first weekend of May to savor authentic Cajun and Creole cuisine and enjoy zydeco and Cajun music. Are you ready to dance? ✹

POINTS of INTEREST

NOT TO BE MISSED
Guided tours of the swamps are available in Kraemer, Houma and other towns. In Henderson, take an airboat deep into the Atchafalaya Basin. *basinlanding.com*

SIDE TRIP
Louisiana boasts 2.6 million acres of marshland, and you can see a largely unspoiled portion on the 180-mile Creole Nature Trail. Starting at Sulphur (about 80 miles west of Lafayette), take Highway 27 south through the Sabine National Wildlife Refuge. At Holly Beach, continue east along the Gulf Coast on Highways 27/82, amid stands of ancient live oaks on the way to Creole, where the route veers sharply northward on Highway 27, then follows Highway 14 north and west to Lake Charles.

NEARBY ATTRACTION
The French Quarter, New Orleans

▼

Stands of cypress trees rise out of the Louisiana swamp.

▼ *At a scenic overlook near Cove Road in Accident, Maryland, bright red barns and rich fall colors are a feast for the eyes.*

Maryland

STORY AND PHOTOS BY
PAT AND CHUCK BLACKLEY

HISTORIC NATIONAL ROAD

TRAVEL THROUGH TIME ON THE PATH OF STAGECOACHES AND SOLDIERS ALONG AMERICA'S OLDEST INTERSTATE HIGHWAY.

WHETHER YOU WANT TO ESCAPE to high elevations to beat the summer heat or take in stunning fall foliage, a drive along the National Road in Maryland is always rewarding. Anyone who is interested in outdoor recreation or early American history will marvel at the hidden treasures in the state's western mountains.

Our 41-mile journey began on Alternate Route 40 in Cumberland, which has served as a departure point for travelers since the mid-1700s. In 1806, Congress authorized construction of a national road to improve the old Cumberland Road route and provide access to the Ohio River Valley. It was the first interstate highway built with federal government money.

Outside the city of Cumberland, The Narrows, a mile-wide valley, or water gap, offers passage through the otherwise impervious Allegheny Mountains. It's fascinating to imagine all the stagecoaches and Conestoga wagons that passed through here as pioneer Americans ventured westward in search of land and opportunity.

We had to smile when we saw the 1830s LaVale Toll Gate House. It's no longer in service, but former toll rates are posted.

In Frostburg, charming shops and restaurants await. We were entertained

POINTS of INTEREST

LENGTH
41 miles

NOT TO BE MISSED
The Great Allegheny Passage, a 150-mile recreational trail between Cumberland, Maryland, and Pittsburgh, Pennsylvania. *thegreatallegheny passage.com*

The Western Maryland Scenic Railroad, from Cumberland to Frostburg and back.

FUN FACT
The old National Road is an ancient footpath first forged by Native Americans, then traipsed by explorers and militiamen into the unmapped lands beyond the Appalachians. This historic route was designated a National Scenic Byway in 2003.

NEARBY ATTRACTION
Harpers Ferry National Historic Park, Harpers Ferry, West Virginia

▼

The Youghiogheny Scenic & Wild River lives up to its name.

by the gigantic turntable in the rail yard near the depot and the about-face it provides to the Western Maryland Scenic Railroad steam engines.

Continue driving through the rural countryside to Grantsville, called Little Crossings in Colonial times. Here we found Spruce Forest Artisan Village, where you can watch artists working in their studios.

All the sightseeing might make you hungry for a meal at the Penn Alps Restaurant and Craft Shop, housed in a former stagecoach stop, the Little Crossings Inn. Later, visit Stanton's Mill, a restored gristmill built in 1797.

West of Grantsville, turn south at the intersection with Highway 219 to visit the small historic town of Accident. A bit farther south, the beauty of Swallow Falls State Park, with trails through old-growth forests that lead to tumbling waterfalls, is the perfect place to end the drive. ●

The Drane House, a log cabin built in 1798 in Accident.

The Natchez Trace Parkway Bridge is a concrete double arch span in Franklin, Tennessee.

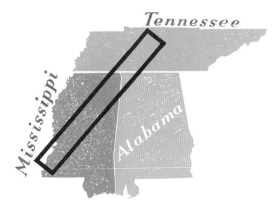

STORY BY **DONNA B. ULRICH**
PHOTOS BY **LARRY ULRICH**

NATCHEZ TRACE PARKWAY

THIS TIMEWORN PATH UNVEILS THE SCENIC APPEAL AND FASCINATING HISTORY OF THE OLD SOUTH.

LIKE ITS EASTERN COUSIN the Blue Ridge Parkway, the Natchez Trace Parkway winds through centuries of history, taking visitors through countryside and cities, past battlefields and barns. "Trace" is from the French for a line of footprints or animal tracks.

In use since pre-Columbian times, the trail was followed first by Native Americans seeking hunting and trading grounds, and later by early European and American explorers and immigrants. Today the 444-mile parkway runs from just south of Nashville, Tennessee, to the city of Natchez, Mississippi.

Though much of the original trail is now unrecognizable, the parkway awaits modern-day explorers. There are no commercial vehicles allowed, making it a slow, relaxing journey.

Years ago we traveled the Natchez Trace for almost a week, inhaling the sights as well as the fragrance of spring lilacs on dewy mornings. Off the main parkway, side roads provide access to remnants that Native Americans, immigrants and armies left behind. Among the witnesses to America's fascinating past are archaeological sites, sunken roads, Civil War battlefields and memorials, historic

POINTS of INTEREST

LENGTH
444 miles

WORDS TO THE WISE
Observe the 50 mph speed limit, which is strictly enforced. When driving, be on the lookout for bicyclists and deer; when hiking, beware of ticks, snakes and poison ivy.

SIDE TRIP
The Hermitage, Andrew Jackson's white-columned home and site of his tomb, covers 1,120 acres and includes a 25,000-square-foot visitor center. Inside his residence, visitors will find original artwork, furniture, personal items and more.

NEARBY ATTRACTIONS
Vicksburg National Military Park, Vicksburg, Mississippi; Mississippi Petrified Forest, Flora; Country Music Hall of Fame, Nashville, Tennessee; Helen Keller Home, Tuscumbia, Alabama

▼
Vicksburg National Military Park honors a decisive Civil War battle.

plantations and Southern towns with lavish antebellum Victorian homes.

On a side road near Natchez, Emerald Mound was built more than two centuries before Columbus landed in America, and is the second-largest ceremonial earthwork in the U.S. This mound, like others in the South and Midwest, is thought to have been a center for religious and social events.

Another excursion took us to Vicksburg, a key Civil War site. We silently toured past rows of cannons. We gazed with respect and awe at the USS *Cairo*, a resurrected ironclad warship at its final resting place as a museum along the Mississippi River.

On the Natchez Trace, you'll discover a fascinating history as old as the dirt under your feet. Along the way, amid exceptional scenery, you may even sense the strength of the settlers who set our country on its zigzag path to the present. ✿

▼
Lake Lee in Tombigbee State Park, Mississippi, is worth a stop.

The Bodie Island Lighthouse at sunset, Cape Hatteras National Seashore.

STORY BY **PAULETTE ROY**
PHOTOS BY **PAUL REZENDES**

OUTER BANKS SCENIC BYWAY

NORTH CAROLINA'S ROUTE 12 BOASTS 200 MILES OF COASTAL CHARM AND A RICH PAST.

THE OUTER BANKS OF NORTH CAROLINA are a narrow string of barrier islands located a few miles out, with white beaches, shifting dunes, effervescent surf, picturesque fishing piers and five historic lighthouses—a winning formula that keeps us coming back!

We approach traveling east through central North Carolina on Highway 64, driving through Roanoke Island and running right into north-south Route 12, a nearly 200-mile-long road spanning the Outer Banks. We opt to turn south, and for long stretches, the narrow road bordered by sand dunes

is the only barrier between the expanse of the Atlantic Ocean and Pamlico Sound. All around us, the interplay of ocean, sand and wind creates an ever-changing landscape.

At Pea Island, a crucial feeding and resting habitat for migratory birds, we see an amazing avian array as we hike the trails. It's a breezy day, so we check the famous windsurfing spot, Canadian Hole between Avon and Buxton.

Our trip isn't complete without sunrise and sunset photos at the Bodie Island and Cape Hatteras lighthouses. At the southern terminus of Route 12,

POINTS of INTEREST

LENGTH
About 200 miles

FUN FACTS
Fishing season never ends, so take some time to find your inner angler. This is known as one of the best places to catch a half-ton marlin!

For nearly 150 years, the towering striped lighthouse at Cape Hatteras has warned sailors away from dangerous shoals. Over time, shifting sands and rolling swells came to threaten the 208-foot beacon, the tallest brick lighthouse in the country. In 1999 it was moved about half a mile to protect it from the encroaching sea. Visitors can climb to the top from mid-April through mid-October.

WORDS TO THE WISE
Keep your car on the road and on paved pull-offs; if you try to park on the shoulder, you'll almost certainly get stuck in the sand. Swim only where lifeguards are on duty.

Footprints in the sand at Pea Island National Wildlife Refuge.

a 40-minute free ferry takes us to Ocracoke Island Lighthouse.

Eventually we head north, past Whalebone Junction, and turn into Jockey's Ridge State Park, the tallest natural sand dune system in the eastern U.S. Families explore dunes and fly kites, while more adventurous folks sandboard and hang glide.

At Nags Head Woods Preserve, a maritime forest, we stroll quietly among the trees and freshwater ponds. Refreshed, we continue north to Kill Devil Hills and the Wright Brothers National Memorial, a must for history buffs and aviation enthusiasts.

Finally, at the northernmost end of Route 12, the 162-foot-tall red brick Currituck Beach Lighthouse beckons. All who climb its 220 steps earn a drink of the gorgeous panoramic view. It's the perfect place to reflect on the overabundance of beauty in North Carolina's Outer Banks. ●

The Roanoke Marshes Lighthouse can be found at the east end of Manteo.

STORY BY
LOUIS BUTTINO

CHEROKEE FOOTHILLS BYWAY

THE CAROLINA MOUNTAINS AND SURROUNDING WILDERNESS OFFER SUPERB FALL COLOR FOR ROAD TRIPPERS.

OUR THREE-CAR CARAVAN hopped on South Carolina Highway 11, known as the Cherokee Foothills National Scenic Byway, north of Spartanburg and headed west. The "Upstate Voyagers" range in age from 56 to 77, with five septuagenarians. We are a no-quit, no-complaints, adventure-loving group of travelers.

Lush orchards lined both sides of the road until we passed Gowensville. We admired the pastoral roadside greenery; rows upon rows of peach trees clung to their leafy cover.

From here, the colors started to change to the yellow, orange and early reds of autumn as we slowly gained altitude. To the north of Highway 11, we could glimpse Hogback Mountain with a patch of sheer vertical granite exposed. All along the byway, we were shadowed by the southernmost peaks of the imposing Blue Ridge Mountains.

Next, we made our much-anticipated stop at the MacGregor Orchard for a delicious supply of fresh apples to snack on during our trip. Back on the road, we passed some of South Carolina's nicest state parks.

Jones Gap, Caesars Head and Table Rock all have different diversions to offer, including trout fishing, hiking trails, a scenic overlook, a swimming hole and waterfalls. Caesars Head is connected to Jones Gap, totaling 13,000 pristine wooded acres in the Mountain Bridge Wilderness Area.

Our caravan crossed over the upper stretch of mountain stream-fed Lake Keowee with its clear water. We headed across the North Carolina state line.

Frequently we have taken fall color trips during the second weekend in October to coincide with local arts and crafts fairs. On this trip, however, we scheduled our travels toward the end of the month to catch the foliage closer to its peak.

This was yet another successful trip for the Upstate Voyagers. I am already thinking about next fall's trip to the Carolina mountains. ❦

PAT & CHUCK BLACKLEY

▼
The sun rises on a misty morning at Table Rock State Park.

POINTS of INTEREST

LENGTH
About 130 miles

NOT TO BE MISSED
Victoria Valley Vineyards; waterfalls of the upcountry

FUN FACT
Table Rock is one of 16 South Carolina state parks built by the Civilian Conservation Corps. The park's Historic District is listed on the National Register of Historic Places. *southcarolina parks.com*

NEARBY ATTRACTIONS
Kings Mountain State Park, with a re-created homestead, and Kings Mountain National Military Park, an American Revolution battle-ground, northeast of Gaffney via Route 29; Oconee State Park, north of Walhalla via Route 107

▼

A cozy farm dressed in autumn hues on Route 640.

STORY AND PHOTOS BY
PAT & CHUCK BLACKLEY

BLUE GRASS VALLEY ROAD

TUCKED AWAY IN THE ALLEGHENIES IS A LITTLE-KNOWN HAVEN WHERE VISTAS NEVER FAIL TO COMFORT AND DELIGHT.

FROM OUR HOME in Virginia's Shenandoah Valley, we enjoy making frequent visits to Highland County, often called Virginia's Little Switzerland for its steep mountains, deep valleys and abundant snowfall.

The drive of less than 50 miles can be a challenging trip of hairpin turns and some white-knuckle moments, but our arrival in this little piece of paradise reminds us why the trip is so worth the effort. Located in the Allegheny Mountains, within what's called the Ridge and Valley province

of the Appalachians, Highland County borders West Virginia to the west and the Shenandoah Valley to the east. Named for its lofty altitude, the county has one of the highest average elevations east of the Mississippi.

The region, isolated by mountains, is home to only about six people per square mile. With only a few small towns or hamlets, it is known and loved for its gorgeous scenery and rural charm. While other areas have been overdeveloped, Highland remains much as it was when we were children.

POINTS of INTEREST

LENGTH
About 50 miles

SIDE TRIPS
Framed by the Blue Ridge and Allegheny mountains, the Shenandoah Valley is renowned for its magnificent vistas. The history, art and culture of this region are represented at the Museum of the Shenandoah Valley. In addition to the museum, the site includes the 18th-century Glen Burnie Historic House, home to descendants of Col. James Wood, founder of the city of Winchester, and 6 acres of beautifully landscaped gardens.

At Natural Chimneys Park, the chimneys soaring above the surrounding plain are a remnant of a time, centuries ago, when an ocean covered the Shenandoah Valley, leaving behind these rocks etched by nature. A jousting tournament has been held on the plains below the chimneys since 1821. Modern knights on galloping horses try to spear rings suspended over the 75-yard course in a meadow called the National Jousting Hall of Fame.

▼
Pisgah Church sits quietly among the hills near Hightown.

There are no four-lane highways, no subdivisions, no fast-food restaurants or shopping malls; you are presented with just miles of peaceful countryside and tightly knit farming communities.

We've traveled countless country roads all around the United States and into Canada, but the quiet, winding drive on Blue Grass Valley Road remains our all-time favorite.

Turning off State Route 220 north of the county seat of Monterey, we are met by the wooded hills and pretty farms of Blue Grass Valley Road. The drive begins as Route 642 goes through the village of Blue Grass, then continues on Route 640 for about 15 miles to the intersection with Route 84, having briefly passed through Hightown.

Meandering through the road's namesake, the beautiful Blue Grass Valley, the route reveals breathtaking wide-open vistas that stretch into the

▼
Enjoy bucolic valley farms with bright green pastures.

▼
Sheep graze together near Blue Grass, Virginia.

An afternoon respite in lush grass.

mountains beyond, reminding us of scenery we've found in Wyoming and Montana.

The fence-lined road passes barns and neatly kept farmhouses scattered among the rolling hills and broad pastures tucked in among the wooded mountain ridges.

Cattle and sheep graze in lush meadows and drink from the waters of the Potomac and James rivers. The headwaters for both rivers are located here. According to local legend, there's a barn in Hightown where rain from the roof's north side runs off into the Potomac and rain from its south side runs to the James.

Each season is alluring, especially for photographers like us. Winter's snow-covered landscape provides a tranquil beauty that grips our souls. Spring and summer bring wildflowers, baby farm animals and the farmers working their fields.

In March, the Highland County Maple Festival celebrates syrup season with events like sugar camp tours where you can learn more about the area from the people who live and work here. A fiddlers' convention, farmers market and delicious trout dinners bring us back each summer.

Our favorite season, though, has to be autumn, when the sugar maples that produce Highland's famous syrup in spring turn the most glorious shades of red, yellow and orange, painting this magnificent landscape with vibrance.

An unhurried drive along this soothing country road reminds us of the way life used to be in earlier times. Selfishly, we hope it never changes, so we can continue to enjoy its remote and pristine beauty for years to come. ●

▼

The Bluff Mountain Tunnel is one of 26 tunnels along the parkway, and the only one located in Virginia.

STORY AND PHOTOS BY
PAT & CHUCK BLACKLEY

BLUE RIDGE PARKWAY

THE GORGEOUS 469-MILE ROLLER COASTER IS MORE THAN A SCENIC DRIVE; IT'S THE ADVENTURE OF A LIFETIME!

WE HAVE TRAVELED THE BLUE RIDGE PARKWAY hundreds of times, photographing the uncommon loveliness and historical charm that make it such a popular scenic destination.

Stretching 469 miles, the parkway connects two national parks in the southern Appalachian Mountains. From its northern origin at Virginia's Shenandoah National Park, the parkway follows the crests of the Blue Ridge Mountains south through Virginia and North Carolina for the first 355 miles. It then skirts the southern end of the Black Mountains and winds through the Craggies and the Balsam Mountains before reaching Great Smoky Mountains National Park.

With a maximum speed limit of 45 mph and no commercial vehicles allowed, the parkway offers a peaceful and relaxing drive, with plenty of opportunities to get out of the car and enjoy the scenic views of mountain ranges, forests and farmlands from its many overlooks and trails. There are no commercial signs or billboards to distract drivers from the natural wonder around them. In fact, the planners who designed and built the parkway in the 1930s intended the journey to be more important than the destination.

The road roller-coasters between deep valleys and high peaks, dropping to an elevation of 649 feet at the James River in Virginia and climbing to more than 6,000 feet at Richland Balsam in North Carolina. This wide range in elevation spans many different climate zones that support an incredible variety of plant and animal life.

There are more than 1,400 plant species along the parkway from early spring through late fall. In spring and summer, we love the dazzling floral displays of azaleas, mountain laurel and rhododendrons. In autumn, a wide variety of deciduous trees makes for an unparalleled extravaganza of fall color.

Chance encounters with wildlife are always highlights of our trips, and we've been fortunate to enjoy numerous sightings of white-tailed deer and black bears, as well as foxes, raccoons and other small critters.

POINTS of INTEREST

LENGTH
469 miles

NOT TO BE MISSED
Mabry Mill is an icon on the parkway. Built more than a century ago, the mill embodies the history and spirit of Appalachia. To this day, neighbors gather there to hear folk and mountain music and to see traditional crafts in action.

FUN FACT
Eighty years ago workers cleaned and graded land that would become the first 12½-mile segment of the parkway. Planners envisioned a road that made the journey more important than the destination.

WORDS TO THE WISE
Because of snow and ice, some sections of the parkway may be closed in winter.

SIDE TRIP
Take a driving break and visit lovely, tree-lined Price Lake in North Carolina to rent a canoe. It's the only lake on the parkway that allows boating.

A Blue Ridge sunrise dazzles the eyes and nourishes the soul.

Each year we also look forward to watching the seasonal migration of hawks and other raptors.

When we tire of driving, we hop out of the car and hike one of the parkway's plentiful trails to waterfalls, wildflower meadows or high, rocky summits. One of our favorites is the Tanawha Trail in North Carolina. High atop the trail's Rough Ridge section, a boardwalk crosses the mountain's fragile ecosystem and provides expansive views of the mountains stretched out as far as you can see. In June, this area is spectacular with blooming mountain laurel and rhododendrons, while in October it's ablaze with blueberry heaths that turn a fiery red.

Scotch-Irish, German and English settlers homesteaded this region of the Appalachians. Visitor center exhibits and restored historic structures along the parkway provide opportunities to see how those hearty mountain folk lived and played. You can almost always catch demonstrations of weaving, wood carving and other crafts. And talented musicians with dulcimers, fiddles, banjos and guitars fill the air with lively mountain music during numerous festivals.

On each journey down the parkway, we never fail to experience or glimpse something new. We'll hike a different trail, discover a new waterfall or wildflower meadow, or spot wildlife somewhere we've never seen it before.

And no matter how many sunrises and sunsets we witness from the lofty overlooks, each one is different. It's as if God chooses new shades of reds, pinks, purples and oranges from his infinite color palette to create his daily masterpieces.

For us, the parkway is not just a scenic drive. It's an adventure, a journey back, an exploration of nature. It's an opportunity to escape to the mountains, immerse ourselves in their tranquil beauty, and reflect on nature's magnificent creation. ❧

The well-photographed Mabry Mill invites visitors to the past.

▼
The Blue Ridge Parkway curves through the peaceful meadows of Doughton Park.

"The health of the eye
seems to demand a
horizon. We are never
tired, so long as we can
see far enough."

—RALPH WALDO EMERSON

Northeast

MAINE

VERMONT

NEW HAMPSHIRE

NEW YORK

MASSACHUSETTS

CONNE-
CTICUT

RHODE ISLAND

PENNSYLVANIA

NEW JERSEY

▼
Mount Katahdin stands in the distance as the sun rises above the East Branch Penobscot River near Medway.

Maine

STORY BY **PAULETTE M. ROY**
PHOTOS BY **PAUL REZENDES**

KATAHDIN WOODS

THE SHOWY FALL FOLIAGE OF NORTH-CENTRAL MAINE IS
A MUST-SEE FOR LEAF-PEEPING ENTHUSIASTS.

VIEW MAINE'S HIGHEST MOUNTAIN, raft down a mighty river or explore the state's prettiest inland park as you travel the 89-mile Katahdin Woods & Waters Scenic Byway. You can access the route near its middle from either of the towns of Sherman or Millinocket, so you'll need to backtrack a bit in order to travel the entire route, but it's worth it.

We entered near Sherman and made our way north, as that entails the least amount of backtracking. Every bend in the road opened to another camera-worthy wilderness view of warm reds, yellows and oranges of autumn. The mighty Mount Katahdin, which is Maine's tallest peak at 5,268 feet and the northern terminus of the Appalachian Trail, popped in and out of view. There aren't many amenities along this northern stretch of the byway, but deep woods, lovely lakes and streams, curvy roads, and one spectacular overlook at Ash Hill in Patten shouldn't be missed.

Near the northern end of the scenic byway, we took a slight detour into the Katahdin Woods and Waters National Monument on the eastern side of Baxter State Park. Be aware that there is no monument, though the locals are fond of asking tourists if they found it! These northern roads are rough, and flat tires are not uncommon, as we discovered after heading back south.

Once we backtracked to Sherman and headed west and south into new territory, the East Branch of the Penobscot River paralleled the road near Hay Brook, a small village north of Medway. We made a quick stop at Grindstone Falls, a popular spot to picnic, walk along the river or cast a fishing line. There's even a riverfront campground that's ideal for watching the sun set or rise.

After enjoying a nice blue and pink sunrise on the river, we made our way to Millinocket, the "big" city along the route. We stopped briefly to grab a bite to eat and get supplies. Moose watching

POINTS of INTEREST

LENGTH
89 miles

REST STOPS
From campsites to cottages, Shin Pond Village is a peaceful overnight retreat on the northern end of the scenic byway. *shinpond.com*

Just miles from the south entrance of Baxter State Park, in the New England Outdoor Center, take advantage of River Driver's Restaurant for casual lakeside dining with views of Mount Katahdin.

SIDE TRIPS
Experience the thrill of mild or wild whitewater rafting on the Penobscot River. Penobscot Adventures has tours for all activity levels. *penobscot adventures.com*

Let Katahdin Air give you a bird's-eye view of the beautiful fall foliage and terrain on one of its scenic plane rides. *katahdinair.com*

Maine's logging industry comes alive at the Patten Lumbermen's Museum through displays, photos and thrilling tales. *lumber mensmuseum.org*

▼
A beautiful bend of the Katahdin Woods & Waters Scenic Byway.

is by far one of the area's major outdoor activities. Wander the back roads wherever there are wetlands, and your chances of spotting one are good. Just keep your distance.

Traveling northwest out of Millinocket, we followed signs for Baxter State Park as the byway leaves Routes 11 and 157 behind and continues westward on Millinocket Road between Millinocket and Ambajejus lakes. Both of these large lakes are popular spots

for recreation, including fishing, boating and swimming.

Though we were determined to complete the entire length of the scenic byway, we took a few side roads along the way, including the well-known Golden Road. This rough dirt road, with washboard bumps in places, parallels the byway; a number of crossover roads provide access. It is worth the adventure, but watch for logging trucks.

▼
More interested in lunch than the view, these grazing cows add to the ambiance of the Ash Hill scenic overlook.

▼
Take a selfie at the iconic Pockwockamus Rock near the southern entrance to Baxter State Park.

Brilliant color decorates the banks of the East Branch Penobscot River.

As we headed west, we came to Compass Pond, a favorite moose habitat that boasts Mount Katahdin as a backdrop. An even more spectacular view of the mountain awaited at Abol Bridge over the West Branch of the Penobscot River. Just a few miles down the road is Nesowadnehunk Falls, an often-roaring waterfall on the West Branch of the Penobscot.

Back on the byway and nearing its end, we entered deep woods with brilliant fall foliage arching over the road. Every now and then we would glimpse Mount Katahdin in the distance, looming above all else, although there are other mountains in the park worthy of attention.

When Pockwockamus Rock, the iconic boulder with the words "Keep Maine Beautiful" painted on it, appeared on the right side of the road, we knew we were getting close. There's a small area for safe parking—it seems no tourist is able to pass by without taking at least one selfie with the rock.

A few miles beyond, we reached the end of the byway at the Togue Pond Gate entrance to Baxter State Park. The road continues past the gate (there is an entrance fee to the park), where more adventures and photo opportunities await. If you have time, spend a day visiting the park and hike up one of the smaller mountains. Photographers will want to stroll to Sandy Stream and Stump ponds to capture stunning foliage and wildlife. Plus, every pondside park campground rents canoes and kayaks for you to take a relaxing paddle along a colorful shoreline. It's a splendid way to end a trip. However you end your journey, it will be a trip worth remembering. ◖

▼

Reds, golds and oranges reach as far as the eye can see near Dallas Plantation, Maine.

STORY BY **PAULETTE M. ROY**
PHOTOS BY **PAUL REZENDES**

RANGELEY LAKES SCENIC BYWAY

FOR FALL COLOR WITHOUT THE CROWDS, DISCOVER THE MAJESTIC PEAKS AND DENSE FORESTS OF MAINE.

THE RANGELEY LAKES REGION of Maine offers leaf peepers the perfect alternative to view spectacular foliage and avoid the crowds in the White Mountains across the border in New Hampshire.

Six major lakes comprise the Rangeley Lakes region, plus hundreds of smaller bodies of water and thousands of acres of forests. In the eastern part of the region, the Bigelow Range and Sugarloaf Mountain form a grand backdrop to the lakes.

Our scenic drive begins at Stratton, on the southern end of Flagstaff Lake. Traveling south and west along state Route 16, we pass wetlands.

The first highlight comes with a detour up Quill Hill via Oddy Road for a 360-degree view of the lakes and mountains. To drive up and see the view will cost a small fee of $10 per car.

Though the vista is popular and it's often windy at the top, my husband, Paul, and I once managed to be there alone on a still morning, with the valleys shrouded in fog and the sun bursting through the clouds.

After heading back down the road, we continue on to Rangeley—a rustic resort town on the lake of the same name—to get gas, supplies and lunch. Then we head westward on routes 16 and 4, along the Rangeley Lakes National Scenic Byway to the village of Oquossoc, where we pay a quick visit to the historic 1916 Union Log

POINTS of INTEREST

LENGTH
About 35 miles

SIDE TRIPS
Once a bustling gold mining site, Coos Canyon gives visitors a chance to try their luck panning for glittery nuggets. *cooscanyonrock andgift.com*

Every August for more than 60 years, Harbor Park in Rockland, a historic harbor town along Maine's midcoast, attracts thousands of people to its Lobster Festival for five days of feasting and fun. Here visitors will find 20,000 pounds of fresh lobster, dozens of artisans and vendors, cooking contests, road races, a parade, carnival rides and U.S. Navy ship tours, just to name a few of the exciting events. *mainelobster festival.com*

NEARBY ATTRACTIONS
Washburn-Norlands Living History Center, Livermore; Thorncrag Nature Sanctuary, Lewiston

▼
The Lovejoy Bridge in South Andover was built in 1868.

Church before turning south onto state Route 17.

There are a number of overlooks along the byway worth checking out, but a must-stop is the Height of Land atop Spruce Mountain, near where the Appalachian Trail crosses the road. At Height of Land, there are views of the mountains in western Maine and of Mooselookmeguntic Lake, a tongue-twisting name derived from a native Abenaki word meaning "portage to moose-feeding place."

From here we continue south along Route 17 to Beaver Pond in Franklin, enjoying the stillness of lily pads at the water's edge.

We end our drive at the 500-yard gorge and waterfall at Coos Canyon, on the Swift River in Byron. It's a top spot for picnics and swimming in summer, but on this cool fall day, the brilliant foliage keeps us warm. ❧

▼
Mooselookmeguntic Lake looks both refreshing and calm on a fall day.

A red barn in Charlemont almost upstages the fall foliage behind it.

STORY BY **PAULETTE M. ROY**
PHOTOS BY **PAUL REZENDES**

BERKSHIRE BYWAYS

SPECTACULAR HILLSIDES ABLAZE IN AUTUMN DAZZLE TRAVELERS ON THE ROADS IN WESTERN MASSACHUSETTS.

AS LIFELONG NEW ENGLANDERS, we've had ample opportunity to photograph foliage throughout the years. Although we travel far and wide, we often find some of the best fall foliage within a couple of hours' drive from home. A terrific area is the Berkshire Mountains of western Massachusetts.

From our home in north-central Massachusetts, we head west along Route 2, the famous Mohawk Trail, which is another prime scenic byway for fall foliage. We continue west, cross the Connecticut River at French King Bridge, and begin our slow, gradual ascent of the rounded-top mountains of the Berkshire Plateau. No craggy, sharp-peaked mountaintops here, but on a clear day, three-state vistas treat us to spectacular hillsides of red, gold, orange, yellow and russet leaves.

After a thrilling descent through the hairpin curve that lies just beyond the western summit of the Hoosac Range, we go through North Adams and head south on Notch Road toward Mount Greylock State Reservation, which was the state's first wilderness park. We pass by old-growth forests on our way to the summit of the 3,491-foot Mount Greylock, the highest peak in Massachusetts. We soak up the 360-degree view of other distant mountains and numerous river valleys below, all ablaze in autumn colors. Since we're on a photo mission, we travel on, but there are many hiking trails on the mountain, including a portion of the Appalachian National Scenic Trail.

Once off the mountain, we take Route 7 south to Pittsfield, where a side trip west via Route 20 brings us to Hancock Shaker Village, a historic village with museum exhibits, a farm and family activities.

After this detour, we continue on Route 7 to the picturesque towns of Lenox, Lee and Stockbridge. Truly the cultural center of western Massachusetts, the trio is host to many theater, dance and music venues, including world-renowned Tanglewood, the summer home of the Boston Symphony Orchestra. In season, you can picnic on the expansive

POINTS of INTEREST

SIDE TRIPS

See the world's largest collection of original art by Norman Rockwell at the Norman Rockwell Museum in Stockbridge. *nrm.org*

In a place like the Berkshires, many country roads lead to gorgeous scenery and New England charm. Take time to explore the Mohawk Trail, which runs from east to west through the northern Berkshires. *mohawktrail.com*

In Mohawk Trail State Forest you'll find a wild terrain of gorges, tumbling brooks, sudden ridges and rocky outcrops, all in a densely mixed forest. Hikers can sample gentle to moderately ambitious trails. Anglers can try their luck for trout. And wildlife watchers will find the woods are alive with wonders.

NEARBY ATTRACTIONS

Historic Deerfield, featuring well-preserved 18th- and 19th-century homes; Natural Bridge State Park, a 550-million-year-old marble formation, North Adams; The Clark Art Institute, Williamstown

▼

The First Congregational Church in Dalton is nestled in ivy.

lawn there and listen to some of the world's greatest musicians perform.

The trio of towns has a bit of literary history, too. Author Edith Wharton's summer home, The Mount, is located in Lenox and is open to the public. Nathaniel Hawthorne wrote *The House of the Seven Gables* while living in a little red cottage in Stockbridge.

A few miles outside of Stockbridge, we come to one of our favorite overlooks: Monument Mountain. This view does require a hike, and although it's less than a mile if you take the shortest and steepest ascent, we usually plan to spend at least two hours to truly enjoy the adventure.

Once back in the van, we continue south along Route 7 through Great Barrington, following the valley's farmlands through Sheffield, where we make a quick visit to Lime Kiln Farm Wildlife Sanctuary. There's a magnificent view of Mount Everett from the walking trails that amble through the sanctuary's old fields and pastures. The farm is home to

more than 500 plant species. The hayfields, limestone ridge and conifer forest attract more than 50 species of butterflies and several birds, including pileated woodpeckers and alder flycatchers.

Our final road trip destination is Bartholomew's Cobble, a rare gem of twin rocky knolls created by geologic upheaval. The cobbles are made of quartzite and marble. The bedrock is 100 feet high and is especially known for a large number of fern species. It has such amazing biological diversity that it has been designated a National Natural Landmark. Worthy of a day visit in itself, the property has 5 miles of hiking trails to explore as well as marshes, beaver ponds, small caves, the Housatonic River and Hurlburt's Hill.

At 1,000 feet, Hurlburt's Hill is the highest point in the park and offers a panoramic view of the Massachusetts-Connecticut border and Housatonic River Valley.

Our good times in the Berkshires have only just begun! ❧

The Bissell Covered Bridge spans Mill Brook in Charlemont.

The Cape Cod Highland Lighthouse in Truro, Massachusetts, creates the perfect New England scene.

STORY AND PHOTOS BY
PAUL REZENDES

CAPE COD'S ROUTE 6

SAND DUNES, HIDDEN FORESTS AND OCEAN VIEWS ABOUND ON THIS DRIVE THROUGH THE CAPE.

THERE'S A 25-MILE STRETCH of U.S. Route 6 from the elbow to the tip of Cape Cod that I love. It's difficult to get far on this road, which runs through the Massachusetts towns of Eastham, Wellfleet, Truro and Provincetown, because there's so much beauty to explore—and, for me, to photograph.

On either side of Route 6, you'll find sandy beaches, marshes, dunes, maritime forests and a simply exquisite national seashore, not to mention quaint villages, historic lighthouses and picturesque harbors.

The peninsula narrows to a mere 1.14 miles across at one point and is not more than 5 miles wide along the entire distance. One of my favorite things to do is park just off the highway in Provincetown—P'town, as the locals call it—and hike into the sand dunes. They are quite vast; as popular as the

cape is in summer, I've spent hours there without meeting another person.

There's lots of soft white sand, covered in some places with beach grasses. Within the dunes stand beautiful forests of pitch pine, some so dense they're impassable, while other spots are open and inviting, with a lush carpet of pine needles. Another delightful discovery is that amid all the sand and trees there are small oases of wild blueberry and huckleberry bushes, plus wild cranberry bogs, providing visitors delicious fruit for a quick snack along the way.

I like to visit the dunes in fall, when the leaves of the fruit bushes and cranberry bogs turn a brilliant ruby red. They make a stark contrast to the dark trees and white sands, creating vivid scenes for the photographer and painter willing to hike to them.

POINTS of INTEREST

LENGTH
25 miles

NOT TO BE MISSED
Whale-watching excursions depart from Barnstable Harbor and Provincetown.

FUN FACT
The Cape Cod Baseball League provides the opportunity to enjoy some of the best collegiate talent in the country. Games are free and played daily, from June to mid-August, in nearly every town on the Cape. Many Major League players got their start here.

WORDS TO THE WISE
On summer weekends, expect bumper-to-bumper traffic at Sagamore Bridge. To avoid crowds, visit before July 4 or after Labor Day.

NEARBY ATTRACTIONS
Cape Cod Museum of Natural History, Brewster; Plimoth Plantation, Plymouth; Martha's Vineyard and Nantucket Island

An old fire road at Cape Cod National Seashore.

Most people go to the cape in summer to enjoy the spectacular beaches, many miles of which are protected by the National Park Service. Along with pristine sands, some beaches on the ocean side have sand cliffs that rise close to five stories high. I tend to like quieter, more secluded spots, so I escape from the hubbub of the season at several small, crystal-clear ponds in the pine forests near Truro and Wellfleet.

The phenomenal sunrises over the Atlantic Ocean make it worth the effort to rise early. In the evenings, I head to Cape Cod Bay for the sunsets. Here it's quite a different scene, with miles of salt marshes and tidal flats that seem to go on forever.

I try to get out to the cape in different seasons, but no matter how many times I travel Route 6 from Eastham to Provincetown, I never run out of places to visit and pictures to take. ✿

Cahoon Hollow Beach in Cape Cod National Seashore basks in the sun's glory.

Albany Bridge was built in 1858 to replace a bridge that was destroyed in a storm.

STORY AND PHOTOS BY
PAT & CHUCK BLACKLEY

KANCAMAGUS SCENIC BYWAY

LEAVE THE HUSTLE AND BUSTLE BEHIND AND HEAD OUT TO ONE OF NEW ENGLAND'S MOST STRIKING FALL DRIVES.

AUTUMN AND NEW ENGLAND seem to go together like Thanksgiving and turkey, so we often head north when we're making plans for autumn. And the Kancamagus Scenic Byway in the White Mountains of New Hampshire is one of our favorite destinations.

The Kanc, as it's known locally, winds through the White Mountain National Forest alongside the pristine Swift River. It's a beautiful drive any time of year, but the Kanc is absolutely fabulous in the fall.

The mixed deciduous trees—maple, white birch, beech, black cherry and poplar—with their vivid shades of red, yellow and orange, contrast dramatically with the dark greens of spruce and hemlock. You also stand a good chance of spotting black bears,

deer and the ever-popular moose. The best fall color usually begins during the second week of September at the higher elevations and peaks during the first two weeks of October.

The area's rich history also played a large role in earning the Kanc its designation as an American Scenic Byway. The highway and surrounding mountains are named after some of the area's most famous Native Americans. In the 1600s, Chief Passaconaway united 17 regional tribes to form the Pennacook Confederacy. His grandson, Kancamagus, meaning "the fearless one," was the third and final ruler of this confederacy.

The byway itself began simply as disconnected mountain roads to the small towns of Passaconaway and

Swift River at Rocky Gorge is a terrific spot to stop and take a photo.

POINTS of INTEREST

LENGTH
34.5 miles

FUN FACTS
Named for a Pennacook chief, "The Kanc," as locals call it, rises to an elevation of 2,900 feet, making it one of the highest roadways in the Northeast.

WORDS TO THE WISE
When making the drive on "The Kanc," you'll find no gas stations, no restaurants and no hotels or other businesses. Also, be on the lookout for moose while driving—especially after dusk, when they often cross the road.

NEARBY ATTRACTIONS
The Frost Place, featuring a nature trail and memorabilia of the celebrated poet Robert Frost, near Franconia

Lincoln. The road to Passaconaway was completed in 1837, but the two roads weren't connected between Conway and Lincoln until 1937. The highway, a 34.5-mile section of Route 112 that climbs to nearly 3,000 feet as it crosses the flank of Mount Kancamagus, was completed and opened to through traffic in 1959.

Along the way, it passes a number of interesting historic sites, including the Albany Covered Bridge and the

Russell-Colbrath Homestead. This humble Cape Cod-style farmhouse was built in the early 1830s by Thomas Russell and his son Amzi. The U.S. Forest Service purchased it in 1961 to preserve the historic location and show what it might have been like to earn a living in these mountains 200 years ago. A post and beam barn built in 2003 serves as an interpretive center.

While there's nothing wrong with admiring the scenery from the comfort

▼
The White Mountains and Lily Pond, a popular place to go moose-watching.

▼
New Hampshire's state Highway 112 winds through the unforgettable White Mountains.

One of the highway's many awesome lookout points.

of your car, the highway abounds with enticing opportunities to get out and explore. Several scenic overlooks offer stunning vistas, and there are plenty of picnic areas.

You can also discover a variety of hiking trails—ranging from short and easy to long and strenuous—that lead to beautiful waterfalls, ponds or mountain summits. One of our favorites, Sabbaday Falls Trail, is just a short hike that rewards you with a series of picturesque cascades flowing through a narrow rock flume. We love to seek out secluded spots by the river to sit and drink in the beauty of autumn foliage reflected in the water.

Or we head to Rocky Gorge Scenic Area, where the Swift River plunges through a chasm carved through the rock by runoff from a mile-high glacier in the last ice age. The area features a

large parking lot and a short paved path that leads to a footbridge with an outstanding view up the gorge. Across the bridge the path leads to a mile-long loop around idyllic Falls Pond, which is also a popular fishing area.

While there are no restaurants, motels, gas stations or stores on this truly pristine byway, it does offer six national forest campgrounds. And noncampers will find plenty of lodging and restaurant options in both Conway and Lincoln—along with interesting gift shops and many locally crafted treasures such as wood carvings and copper cupolas.

Autumn in New Hampshire's White Mountains is an experience not to be missed, and the Kancamagus Highway transports us into the heart of that grandeur while leaving intrusions from the modern world behind. ●

STORY AND PHOTOS BY
PAT & CHUCK BLACKLEY

OLD MINE ROAD

DRIVE THIS HISTORIC ROUTE THROUGH THE DELAWARE WATER
GAP TO DISCOVER NEW JERSEY'S SCENIC SIDE.

MAJESTIC VIEWS. HISTORIC SITES. Hiking trails, swimming and fishing. Old Mine Road on the New Jersey side of the Delaware Water Gap National Recreation Area beckons you.

The 1,000-foot-deep Delaware Water Gap is the key passageway through the Appalachian Mountain range between Pennsylvania and New Jersey. Each year about 5 million visitors enjoy the Gap's 70,000-acre national recreation area, the largest in the eastern United States.

The 104-mile Old Mine Road connects incredible fall scenery and recreation that includes hiking a section of the famous Appalachian Trail and boating, picnicking or viewing waterfalls along the Delaware River.

Begin your journey at the Kittatinny Point Visitor Center at the southern end of River Road (which soon becomes Old Mine Road going north). Drive north to Millbrook Village, a re-created farm community from the mid-1800s. With a wagon shop, general store, hotel and church, the village has plenty for visitors to see.

Continue north to take in the view from Kittatinny Mountain via Route 624 and Skyline Drive, a spectacular mountain vista. On a crisp day, fall colors paint a sea of trees as far as the horizon. It's a welcome place to stop and stretch your legs on part of the Appalachian Trail.

Back on Old Mine Road, stop for a picnic and a swim in the river or explore more historic structures. To view additional fall color, detour from that drive and linger in Walpack Center, a small 1800s village that's listed on the National Register of Historic Places. Then it's time to link back up to Old Mine Road again for more adventure. ●

POINTS of INTEREST

LENGTH
104 miles

REST STOPS
Jam to jazz and sleep late at charming Deer Head Inn on the Pennsylvania side of the Gap, northwest of the Kittatinny Point Visitor Center. *deerheadinn.com*

Stop at the rustic Walpack Inn, established in 1949, to indulge in a lovely meal served with its famous brown bread and set against the stunning views of Walpack Valley. *thewalpackinn.com*

SIDE TRIPS
Coppermine Trail, a moderate to difficult 2-mile, one-way trail through the forest along streams and cascades, is part of more than 100 miles of hiking trails in the Delaware Water Gap National Recreation Area. *nps.gov/dewa*

Browse through the handmade items created by artists in the gallery and shop at the Peters Valley School of Craft. Or sign up for a one-day workshop to try blacksmithing, basketry, woodworking, ceramics and more. *petersvalley.org*

Top: Historic ◄ Millbrook Village's Methodist Episcopal Church takes visitors back in time. Bottom: Spend a peaceful day surrounded by fall's glory at Crater Lake on Mount Kittatinny.

▼

A visitor admires the view from an observation deck at Moss Lake.

New York

STORY AND PHOTOS BY
PAT & CHUCK BLACKLEY

CENTRAL ADIRONDACK TRAIL

FOLLOW SCENIC ROUTE 28 FOR SPARKLING LAKES AND
CHARMING MOUNTAIN VILLAGES.

THE ADIRONDACK PARK encompasses the largest area of publicly protected land in the Lower 48 states. Idyllic country roads abound, and you'd be hard-pressed to find an area that isn't scenic.

The state of New York created the park in 1892 out of concern that this magnificent area—with its abundant forests, majestic mountain peaks, and shimmering lakes and rivers—was in danger of being exploited. Two years later, the Adirondack Forest Preserve was established, which made the park a Forever Wild area. This designation means the land is protected under the constitution of New York to preserve it.

Almost half of the park's total 6 million acres is state property, preserved for the public's enjoyment of pursuits such as camping, hiking, biking, swimming, skiing, boating and fishing. The remainder of the land is privately owned and includes farms,

businesses and more than 100 small towns and villages. This is ideal for travelers who relish a wilderness experience, but still appreciate the comforts found in nearby towns.

On one recent fall visit we drove along a 50-mile stretch of state Route 28/28N. This is part of the 150-mile-long Central Adirondack Trail, which is an Adirondack Scenic Byway.

We began at the intersection of Routes 28N and 30 in Long Lake and traveled southwest along a chain of lakes that ends at Old Forge. The trees were magnificent, with their vibrant colors of red, orange and yellow reflecting in the clear lake waters.

The community of Long Lake, one of the oldest in the region, is nestled on the shores of a 14-mile-long lake of the same name. If you wish to stop and soak up the scenery, boat and seaplane tours offer a different perspective.

Seaplanes offer aerial tours of Long Lake.

POINTS of INTEREST

LENGTH
150 miles

WORDS TO THE WISE
Black flies and other insect pests can be numerous, especially in early summer.

SIDE TRIP
The Museum on Blue Mountain Lake tells the history of the Adirondacks region and its people.
theadkx.org

NEARBY ATTRACTION
Lake George Beach State Park, with swimming and picnicking, east of Fort William Henry

We continued south along Routes 28N/30 to Blue Mountain Lake, one of the most beautiful of the approximately 3,000 Adirondack lakes. Set against the backdrop of 3,759-foot Blue Mountain, the scenery is gorgeous. The hamlet of Blue Mountain Lake is home to the Adirondack Lakes Center for the Arts, which hosts concerts, plays and classes. The Blue Mountain Lake Boat Livery offers lake tours and rents all types of vessels, from fishing boats to canoes and paddleboats.

We stayed at the Prospect Point Cottages, one of many lodging choices in the area. It's right on the lake, and the private beach has spectacular views of the water and mountains. Plus, our hosts served a brunch buffet that kept us going until supper!

After visiting Lake Durant, just to the east, we resumed our trip along Route 28 west, past Eagle Lake and Utowana Lake and onward to Raquette Lake. As the largest natural body of water within the park, Raquette Lake is renowned for nearly 100 miles of primarily state-owned shoreline.

In the late 1800s, this area attracted Gilded Age millionaires like Vanderbilt, Carnegie and Morgan who built large summer homes they referred to as camps. One of the grandest, Great Camp Sagamore, is down the road from the hamlet of Raquette Lake.

Route 28 runs along a long chain of eight lakes, called the Fulton Chain, which are known only by number, First through Eighth. We made frequent stops at pullouts and public beaches to admire and photograph the picturesque lakes. We also explored small villages and towns such as Eagle Bay and Inlet before ending our drive in Old Forge.

Like the other lake communities, Old Forge offers plenty of choices for outdoor enthusiasts, plus boat tours and even a scenic chairlift ride for viewing fall color at the McCauley Mountain Ski Resort.

Another popular activity is the fall foliage tour aboard the Adirondack Scenic Railroad.

A drive along Route 28 would be delightful any time of the year, but we found it especially enjoyable in fall. ❧

Blue Mountain Lake is a splendid place to watch the sunset.

STORY AND PHOTO BY
CINDY RUGGIERI

HIGH PEAKS BYWAY

MAP OUT A COURSE FOR ADVENTURE WITH AN AUTUMN BACKDROP IN THE ADIRONDACKS.

NO MATTER WHAT OUTDOOR ACTIVITY you're into—mountain biking, canoeing, camping, fishing or snow skiing—"forever wild" Adirondack Park has it all.

Each season in the Adirondacks has its own recreational appeal, but for me, autumn hiking is awe-inspiring! The park's forest preserve offers more than 6 million acres of breathtaking scenery.

My favorite drive is in the High Peaks region. Jump off Interstate 87 to Route 73 and drive about 40 miles northwest to pretty Saranac Lake. Give yourself plenty of time for stops along the way.

Route 73 winds and curves through a hiker's paradise, with plenty of trailheads along the roadside. Of the 46 mountain peaks in the Adirondacks, all but four are located in this area. Serious hikers who set a goal to hike all of them can be recognized as members of the Adirondack 46ers club.

I always make my first stop at Chapel Pond for a peaceful walk along the shore. The slabs opposite the road are popular spots for rock climbers, with some 700 feet of smooth climbing surface. From here, follow the road north to Keene and make a quick pit stop at the Cedar Run Bakery & Market for baked goods and sandwiches.

On one of our visits my husband and I turned onto Owl's Head Lane, a few miles west of Keene, to take the half-mile hike to the Owl's Head peak. It may have been a short hike, but it was a lot of work going up, climbing over tree roots and rocks.

The payoff was worth the effort—the vistas were spectacular. With only a slight breeze to break up the peace and quiet, we stood in wonder at the mountains around us, bursting with bold autumn colors.

With that memory to treasure, we hiked back down to the road and continued on 73. The road winds along Upper and Lower Cascade Lakes. Pull into the parking area between the lakes for sightseeing, fishing, hiking and paddling on the water.

Whether you end your trip in beautiful Lake Placid or follow Route 86 on to Saranac Lake, this drive is always worth the trip. ●

POINTS of INTEREST

LENGTH
30 miles

WORDS TO THE WISE
Black flies and other insect pests can be numerous, especially in early summer.

SIDE TRIPS
Lake Placid hosted the 1980 Winter Olympics. This winter, take a bobsled ride at the Olympic Sports Complex. *lakeplacid.com*

After dipping into a broad valley, the drive heads into the town of Keene. A side detour from there diverts to the west to the High Peaks Wilderness, where travelers can park and then head out on foot to sample some of the scenery afforded by the 238 miles of hiking trails that lace the area.

NEARBY ATTRACTION
Six Nations Indian Museum, with displays of native crafts, Onchiota, 14 miles north of Saranac Lake

Owl's Head peak is a nice spot for repose.

▼
Women of the Nebraska Amish group travel the back roads amid fall elegance.

STORY AND PHOTOS BY
DOYLE YODER

PENNSYLVANIA ROUTE 655

THE BIG VALLEY LIVES UP TO ITS NAME ON THIS JOURNEY THROUGH AMISH COUNTRY.

CENTRAL PENNSYLVANIA is a land of rural valleys tucked away in the Appalachian Mountains. Probably the most amazing of them all is the Kishacoquillas Valley, or as the Amish call it, the Big Valley.

For an afternoon drive through this idyllic country, start on U.S. Route 22 and turn onto Pennsylvania Route 655 at Mill Creek. You'll wind through a cut in the mountains for a few miles and then you'll come to the opening of the valley.

At 30 miles long and 5 miles wide, the Big Valley is surrounded by mountains, including Stone, Front, Jacks and Back. It's also home to three Amish groups—the Byler, Peachey (or Renno) and Nebraska. Each group is known by the color of their buggy tops: yellow, black and white respectively.

As you proceed north on 655, you will pass some of the tidiest Amish farms to be found anywhere. With so many farms along the roads, you can imagine that this is what the area must have looked like in the 1800s.

Fall is a fantastic time to visit. The Amish are out in the fields with their draft horses, gathering the corn into shocks. Mountains stand along either side of the valley ablaze in fall color, and the road runs parallel to all this country beauty.

As you drive along 655, you are sure to find a farm stand with fresh produce or an artisan's workshop. The first town on this route is Allensville, with small shops catering to the locals as well as tourists. In Allensville, stop by the Kishacoquillas Valley Historical Society for an overview of Big Valley history. The two-story building is a relic—it was built in 1838. The museum preserves 150 years of Amish history. Tour an 1830 Pennsylvania bank barn

POINTS of INTEREST

NOT TO BE MISSED

The toil of summer and fall deserve a festive nod. In the Big Valley, the fun takes place during Harvestfest on the first Friday and Saturday in October. Festivities include carriage rides, a quilt raffle and more. *visitbigvalley.com*

FUN FACT

In the 1700s, the Big Valley was home to several Native American tribes. The legacy of Chief Kishacoquillas of the Shawnee lives on throughout the area. In fact, the valley between Jacks Mountain and Stone Mountain was named for him.

WORDS TO THE WISE

Bring a cooler to store foods purchased at roadside stands, but note that most of them are closed on Sunday for observance of the Sabbath.

SIDE TRIP

Poe Valley State Park offers 3 miles of beautiful fall trails that connect to Bald Eagle State Forest. *dcnr.state.pa.us/stateparks*

An Amish man and his son sell produce at the market in Belleville.

filled with wagons, sleds and other farm tools used by the Amish.

The next town is Belleville, which is the biggest in the valley. If you make your trip on Wednesday be sure to stop at the Belleville Livestock Auction, which is on the northeast side of town. This farmers market is a busy place and the hub of this rural community.

As you pull into the parking lot you'll see yellow-, white- and black-topped buggies mixed in with cars. From March through November local vendors sell their wares, including produce, eggs, flowers and whoopie pies (also known as moon pies). My advice to you: Take a quick tour of the market before buying. Who knows what treasures you'll find at the next booth?

If you'd like to see the valley from a mountain's point of view, take a drive on East Back Mountain Road, which travels through Barrville; or Front Mountain Road, which can be accessed from Route 655 north of Airydale, near the southern tip of the valley. One of my favorite routes is Jacks Mountain/Wills Road, which leads to a summit overlooking the valley. There you'll see a patchwork of quaint farms in the shadow of the surrounding mountains.

Escape to Pennsylvania's Big Valley, where simple is better, and neighborly folks greet you like an old friend. ❦

▼

Tidy farms and autumn's flare make this drive enchanting.

Vermont's country roads reveal a bounty of picture-perfect moments like this.

STORY AND PHOTOS BY
PAT & CHUCK BLACKLEY

SCENIC ROUTE 100 BYWAY

FALL IN LOVE WITH THE COLOR, CHARACTER AND ALLURE OF THE GREEN MOUNTAIN STATE.

WE WILL ADMIT TO HAVING A LOVE AFFAIR with Vermont. Over the years, we've explored nearly every highway and rural road in the state. But we often find ourselves returning to one particular road, because it includes most everything we adore about this New England gem.

Much of this journey follows the Scenic Route 100 Byway, which runs through the center of Vermont along the full length of the Green Mountain range. All of the scenic sites you picture—quaint villages, country stores, covered bridges and neat farms—can be found on this road, with a few side trips.

You could do our 160-mile drive in a few hours. But with so much to see, try devoting at least two days.

Every season is beautiful here, but you'll see excellent scenery in autumn. With its abundant sugar maple trees,

Vermont has the most vibrant fall foliage imaginable, plus many homes and storefronts are decorated with cheerful harvest displays.

Begin the journey in Manchester. Besides its charming town center that boasts lovely 19th century architecture, Manchester also has a number of lodging and dining options, making it an enjoyable place to explore and stay overnight.

The next morning, hop on Route 11, head east over the mountains for 16 miles and admire the views of the Green Mountain National Forest. Stay on Route 11 for a side trip when you reach the intersection with Route 100 at Londonderry.

After 14 miles, stop in the cute town of Chester to check out the interesting shops and buildings surrounding its village green. Then take Route 35 south for 7 miles to reach the tiny hamlet of

POINTS of INTEREST

LENGTH
160 miles

NOT TO BE MISSED
Honora Winery, Jacksonville; Jamaica State Park; Warren Covered Bridge

WORDS TO THE WISE
Book reservations early for fall foliage tours and accommodations. Mountain roads may be closed in winter. Some attractions are seasonal.

SIDE TRIPS
Billings Farm & Museum, a working dairy in Woodstock, offers tours and demonstrations that depict 19th century rural life. *billings farm.org*

Back roads in the Mad River Valley offer rustic covered bridges, stonewalls, pretty farms and mountain vistas. The tiny town of Warren has a country store with a great deli, and Waitsfield has many cozy inns. *madriver valley.com*

During autumn, visit Jenne Farm near Reading, considered the most photogenic spot in Vermont. Take Route 106 south out of Woodstock to Jenne Road.

▼

Horses soak up the sun in a picturesque pasture near Waitsfield.

Grafton. In an effort to preserve the rural Vermont way of life, a nonprofit foundation bought and restored many of the buildings in this 19th century town, including the historic Grafton Inn. The handsome buildings along Main Street house shops, galleries and museums.

Return to Londonderry and head north on Route 100. Soon you'll arrive in Weston, a town with a tree-lined green, museums, galleries and plenty of shops, including the iconic Vermont Country Store.

Continuing north through the village of Ludlow, splendid views abound along the Okemo Valley. After passing a series of mountain lakes, bear right onto Route 100A to visit the President Calvin Coolidge State Historic Site, his boyhood home and birthplace, in Plymouth Notch.

Follow Route 100A for 6 miles, and then turn right onto Route 4 and travel 8 miles farther to Woodstock, one of the prettiest villages in New England. Elegant homes, little white churches and a bustling shopping area surround the village green.

While you're in Woodstock stop by Vermont's only national park, the Marsh-Billings-Rockefeller National

▼
Reflections of autumn shimmer on a mill pond in the village of Weston.

▼
The sun sets on a cool autumn day at Jenne Farm, one of the most photographed farms in Vermont.

▼

An eye-catching Baptist church in Ludlow graces the town green.

Historical Park. Visit the mansion there that was once home to George Perkins Marsh, father of the American conservation movement, and later Frederick Billings, who advocated for the establishment of Yosemite National Park. An 1895 carriage barn houses the visitor center, and the formal gardens and more than 20 miles of wooded trails are a pleasure to walk through.

Driving around Woodstock will reward you with pristine country scenery. This is where we saw our first Vermont moose!

Return to Route 100 via Route 4 and climb into the mountains to reach Killington, the state's largest ski area. Take a gondola ride for panoramic views. Farther down the road, Gifford Woods State Park holds one of Vermont's few remaining stands of old-growth hardwood trees.

Descending the mountains, the route travels through the bucolic White River Valley, dotted with red barns, dairy farms and peaceful small towns like Rochester.

The valley ends north of Granville, and here the road narrows as it winds 6 miles through the Granville Gulf Reservation, a densely forested wilderness. Make sure you stop and view Moss Glen Falls as it tumbles down 80 feet.

A drive through rural Vermont is like traveling back to yesteryear, and in fall it's magical. The weather is cool and crisp with a hint of woodsmoke in the air, and foliage glows. Cornstalks and pumpkins adorn porches, and shops are filled with friendly folks sipping apple cider. Life doesn't get much better than this. ●

Grist Mill Covered Bridge spans Brewster River in the village of Jeffersonville.

STORY BY **PAULETTE M. ROY**
PHOTOS BY **PAUL REZENDES**

VERMONT ROUTE 108

FIND MOUNTAIN VIEWS AND STUNNING HUES ALONG THIS
ROAD WITH A STORIED PAST.

WE TEND TO ROAM, mostly away from crowds if we can manage it, and that's how we came upon a 17.3-mile portion of Route 108 in Vermont that travels from Stowe to Jeffersonville through a narrow mountain pass known as Smugglers' Notch.

Considered by many to be Vermont's most dramatic road, Route 108 travels through Mount Mansfield State Forest and over Mount Mansfield. At 4,393 feet, the peak is the highest in Vermont. This drive winds around boulders that jut into the country road beneath 1,000-foot cliffs, narrowing to one lane in sections. It is definitely not for the faint of heart, and beeping your horn is essential around the curves. It is so steep (an intense 18% grade) that the road is not plowable, and therefore it's closed in late fall and winter.

The name Smugglers' Notch comes from the road's infamous history. Smugglers used it to bring embargoed goods into Canada during the War of 1812. Later, fugitive slaves crossed this deep, narrow mountain pass to find freedom in the North. The path graduated to a carriage road in 1894, and the present paved route dates from around 1910. During Prohibition, bootleggers used it to move contraband liquor into the United States.

Most travelers begin their journey on the scenic byway at Stowe. You'll find shops, restaurants, lodging, museums, historic sites and art centers along the first several miles. There is much to see and do along the way, so plan to spend several hours.

Consider a jaunt down the Stowe Recreation Path, which parallels the road and has several access points where you can stretch your legs by strolling through cornfields, green meadows, and along the West Branch of Little River.

Perhaps the most popular side trip is the 4-mile Auto Toll Road at Stowe Mountain Resort. You can drive to the summit of Mount Mansfield for sweeping views of the Adirondacks. Many people opt to take a gondola ride up the mountain for a bird's-eye view.

POINTS of INTEREST

LENGTH
17.3 miles

NOT TO BE MISSED
Vermont Ski and Snowboard Museum, Stowe

FUN FACT
Stowe's alpine cachet was helped by the arrival, more than half a century ago, of an Austrian family named Von Trapp—the real-life inspiration behind the popular musical *The Sound of Music.* Just a few miles north and west of the village, off Route 108, the Trapp Family Lodge commands a view of meadows and mountains that might have been imported from the Tyrol, along with the familiar strains of music.

SIDE TRIPS
A quieter, more peaceful and contemplative exploration of fields, forests, ponds, rivers and farmlands awaits the adventurous traveler who is willing to take the not-so-beaten path through the surrounding communities of Cambridge, Fletcher, Bakersfield and Enosburg. These storied towns are home to many historic sites.

▼
Wagons and old barns on the route are part of the fall scenery.

Across from the entrance to Stowe Mountain Resort, you'll find the Barnes Civilian Conservation Corps building now repurposed as the Smugglers' Notch Visitor Center. Linger over the exhibits and the educational programs or ramble along a boardwalk through wetlands. There's also a trailhead for the Long Trail, one of the oldest long-distance hiking trails in the U.S.

Once back on Route 108, you enter the deep woods of Mount Mansfield State Forest and begin the climb up the mountain, arriving at the entrance to Smugglers' Notch State Park. Wild and rugged, it makes a great base camp for exploring the area, and there are several camping options.

From the entrance, the road continues its winding, steep ascent to its namesake, Smugglers' Notch. We stopped at Big Spring, which has a picnic area and leads to rocks with names like Elephant's Head.

From this point begins the sharp descent along breathtaking curves edged with boulders and cliffs through colorful forests. About 3 miles from

Elephant's Head, Smugglers' Notch Resort is a popular family destination with year-round activities.

Route 108 eventually levels out in the village of Jeffersonville along the Lamoille River, for a totally different experience from Stowe. Before entering the village, we stopped to photograph the Grist Mill Covered Bridge spanning the Brewster River on Canyon Road. Built in the 19th century, it was added to the National Register of Historic Places in 1974.

The drive continues north to the Canadian border, but from here we usually take advantage of several country roads off Route 108 to view beautiful farm landscapes with Mount Mansfield as a backdrop. As thrilling as it is to drive along the highway (and it's worth going in both directions at least once), the contrast between the mountain's alpine grandeur and the pastoral scenes of the Lamoille Valley never ceases to take our breath away.

We never know which bend in the road will reward us with a spectacular view. We've had some great surprises! ▪

▼
Camel's Hump, the bumpy peak in the background, is part of the Green Mountain range.

"**Beauty, spiced with wonder, is the greatest lure to travel.**"

—CONFUCIUS

Farms awaken at the foot of Mount Mansfield in Vermont.